BEARINGS

Getting our bearings again in the light of the Gospel

with contributions from
**Peter Adam : Dave Andrews
Helen Beazley : Mark Delaney
Ross Farley : Greg Manning
Charles Ringma**

edited by
Helen Beazley and Dave Andrews

WIPF & STOCK · Eugene, Oregon

Wipf and Stock Publishers
199 W 8th Ave, Suite 3
Eugene, OR 97401

Bearings
Getting our Bearings Again in the Light of the Gospel
By Andrews, Dave and Beazley, Helen
Copyright©2011 by Andrews, Dave
ISBN 13: 978-1-61097-854-5
Publication date 2/1/2012
Previously published by Last First Networks, 2011

Introduction to Dave Andrews for the 2012 Dave Andrews Legacy Series

I KEPT seeing this guy on the shuttle bus - long hair, graying beard, a gentle 60's-70's feel to him. He seemed thoughtful, intense, friendly, and quiet, like he had a lot on his mind, as did I. Even though I saw him nearly every time I boarded the shuttle bus, we didn't speak beyond him smiling and saying, "G'day" and me nodding and saying, "Hey" as we boarded or disembarked.

It was my first time at Greenbelt, a huge festival about faith, art, and justice held every August in the UK. I had always heard great things about the event and so was thrilled when I was invited to speak. I was just as thrilled to get a chance to hear in person some musicians and speakers I had only heard about from a distance, so I went through the program and marked people I wanted to be sure not to miss.

It was near the end of the conference when a friend told me to be sure to catch an Australian fellow named Dave Andrews. "I've never heard of him," I said. "Oh, he's a force of nature," my friend said. "Kind of like Jim Wallis, Tony Campolo, and Mother Teresa rolled up into one." How could I not put a combination like that in one of the last free slots on my schedule?

I arrived at the venue a few minutes late and there he was, the bearded guy from the bus. Thoughtful, intense, and friendly, yes - but *quiet* he was not. He was nearly exploding with passion - passion and compassion, in a voice that ranged from fortissimo to fortississimo to furioso. How could a guy churning with so much hope, love, anger, energy, faith, fury, and curiosity have been so quiet and unassuming on the bus?

He was a force of nature indeed, evoking from his audience laughter, shouts, amens, reverent silence, and even tears before he was done. He spoke of justice, of poverty, of oppression, of solidarity across religious differences, of service, of hope, of celebration, of the way of Jesus.

As I listened, I wanted to kick myself. *This is the most inspiring talk I've heard at this whole festival. Why did I miss all those opportunities to get to know this fellow on the bus? Now the festival is almost over and I've missed my chance!*

Later than evening, I boarded the shuttle bus for the last ride back to my hotel, and there sat Dave and his wife, Ange. I didn't miss my chance this time. I introduced myself and they reciprocated warmly.

I was a largely unknown American author at the time and hardly known at Greenbelt, much less in Australia, so I'm quite certain Dave and Ange had never heard of me. But they couldn't have been kinder, and as we disembarked, he pulled two books from his backpack and told me they were a gift.

The next day when I flew home from Heathrow, I devoured them both on the plane. First, I opened *Not Religion, But Love* and read it through from cover to cover. Then I opened *Christi-anarchy* and couldn't put it down either. When my plane landed, I felt I had been on a spiritual retreat . . . or maybe better said, in a kind of spiritual boot camp!

Things I was thinking but had been afraid to say out loud Dave was saying boldly and confidently. Ideas I was very tentatively considering he had already been living with for years. Complaints and concerns I only shared in highly guarded situations he was publishing from the housetops. Hopes and ideals I didn't dare to express he celebrated without embarrassment.

I think I gave him a copy of one or two of my books as well, and I guess he was favorably impressed enough that we stayed in touch and a friendship developed. I discovered that we were both songwriters as well as writers, that we both had a deep interest in interfaith friendships, that we both had some critics and we both had known the pain of labeling and rejection.

Since then, whatever he has written, I've been sure to read . . . knowing that he speaks to my soul in a way that nobody else does.

We've managed to get together several times since our initial meeting in England, in spite of the fact that we live on opposite sides of the planet. We've spoken together at a few conferences on both hemispheres, and I had the privilege of visiting him in Brisbane. I've seen the beautiful things he has been doing in a particularly interesting and challenging neighborhood there, walking the streets with him, meeting his friends, sensing his love for that place and those people. He's been in my home in the US as well, and we've been conspiring for some other chances to be and work together in the future.

In my speaking across North America, I frequently refer to Dave's work, but until now, his books have been hard to come by. That's why I'm thrilled to introduce this volume to everyone I can in North America.

Yes, you'll find he's one part Tony Campolo, one part Jim Wallis, and one part Mother Teresa, a force of nature, as I was told.

You'll also find he is a serious student of the Bible and a serious theological sage — the kind of reflective activist or thinker-practitioner that we need more of.

In a book like *Christi-anarchy*, he can boldly and provocatively unsettle you and challenge you. Then in a book like *Plan Be*, he can gently and pastorally encourage and inspire you. Like the central inspiration of his life, he is the kind of person to confidently turn over tables in the Temple one minute and then humbly defend a shamed and abused woman from her accusers the next.

You'll see in Dave's writings that he is highly knowledgeable about poverty, ecology, psychology, sociology, politics, and economics . . . not only from an academic standpoint, but also from a grassroots, experiential level. His writing on these subjects grows from what he has done on the ground . . . for example, nurturing a community network that is training young adults to live and serve among the poor, supervising homes for adults who are learning to live with physical and psychiatric disabilities, encouraging small businesses to hire people who others would consider unemployable and developing a non-profit solar energy co-op for local people.

Dave's writings and friendship have meant so much to me. I consider him a friend and mentor. Now I am so happy that people across North America can discover him too.

You'll feel as I did — so grateful that you didn't miss the chance to learn from this one-of-a-kind, un-categorizable, un-containable, wild wonder from Down Under named Dave Andrews.

Brian D. McLaren
author/speaker/activist (brianmclaren.net)

TABLE OF CONTENTS

Introduction to Dave Andrews for the 2012 Dave Anderws Legacy Series

Introduction   **1**
Helen Beazley and Dave Andrews

Navigating the Meanings of Being a 'Christian'   **11**
Mark Delaney

Evangelism in a Pluralist Society   **35**
Ross Farley

An Evangelical Approach to Interfaith Engagement   **49**
Dave Andrews

Liberation Theologians Speak to Evangelicals   **99**
Charles Ringma

Supporting HIV Prevention as People of Faith   **157**
Greg Manning and Dave Andrews

Australia – Whose Land?   **179**
Peter Adam

Antidote for a Poisoned Planet?   **203**
Helen Beazley

INTRODUCTION

Helen Beazley and Dave Andrews

Many of us have encountered and been changed by the Gospel of Jesus. We believe that through us, in the midst of the cataclysmic dilemmas of the Twenty First Century, the world can encounter and be changed by the Gospel of Jesus. We seek to find and follow Christ's direction in the work of spiritual, social, economic, political and environmental transformation. We look to Jesus for our bearings.

But there are problems. Sometimes, when we move from a personal and private faith to the public arena, and look to the Bible for guidance in understanding and responding to the issues demanding our attention, we are often too incapacitated by the momentum of a culturally masculine, middle class, white, western heritage to see what God may be telling us at this time in history through Scriptures. Other times our *God complex* – our absolute certainty that we know how Jesus wants us to respond to situations of need – can rush us to simplistic solutions and damaging courses of action.

The title of this collection is *Bearings: Getting our bearings again in light of the Gospel*. Bearings, as we know, is a navigational term. A sailor will want to know the direction of an object relative to his vessel, to reach that object or perhaps to avoid it. Wrong bearings, and a sailor could crash into rocks or miss her destination. In common usage bearings can take on a metaphorical dimension, referring to our position in reference to other ways of being and believing outside ourselves. How we position ourselves in relation to 'the other'. Sailors got their bearings in various ways throughout history, for example, nautical almanacs, radio waves, or satellites. This essay collection looks to Jesus, and the Scriptures he held as sacred, to find our bearings. But how do we engage with our sacred Scriptures to find our bearings?

The writers of these collected essays give us a way forward.

First, we must engage with the world that God so loves (John 3:16), and read the Bible in light of that engagement. A joke lampooning economists is currently doing the rounds: "Ah, it may work in practice, but does it work in theory?" So often our gut theories about the poor, the disdained, the disempowered, are theories formed without authentic engagement with those in the world who are poor, disdained or disempowered. We need to start with practice and seek theological insight that works in practice, rather than God-theories that fall apart on the ground. Practising the Kingdom of God is the initial step in getting our bearings and can start to undo our unhelpful stereotypes, simplistic theologies and pat answers.

Many of the writers have done this. They have put their hand to the wheel, whether it is working with the poor and people living with HIV, practising evangelism in politically and culturally sensitive contexts, or involvement in grassroots sustainability initiatives. They read the Bible as practitioners rather than onlookers, seeking an orientation true to the God and Christ of mercy, grace, compassion and justice.

For example, Mark Delaney makes sense of the procession of claims about who is a Christian that have influenced his faith journey in *Navigating the Meanings of Being a 'Christian'*. A momentary but life changing encounter with a poor man in India led Mark to re-examine everything he understood about the Gospel, and shines a light on the often contradictory beliefs found across the church community about who should bear the name 'Christian'.

In *Evangelism in a Pluralist Society* Ross Farley applies his experience of evangelism in sensitive contexts to a careful review of evangelism in the New Testament. He finds that much of what we call evangelism bears little relationship to the Gospel and Acts of the Apostles and offers a workable reorientation to evangelism consistent with the approach of Jesus and the Apostles.

On the subject of HIV epidemics, Greg Manning and Dave Andrews have joined the struggle to reduce HIV infection rates and witnessed the stigmatisation of vulnerable people that comes from invoking superficial pronouncements based on poorly applied Christian moral teaching. In *Supporting HIV Prevention as People of Faith*, they consider the Sermon on the Mount as a valuable source of instruction in dealing compassionately and effectively with people vulnerable to HIV infection.

Second we can deliberately read the Bible from other perspectives. To look at the Good News with fresh eyes, we need help to overcome our inherited prejudices. We can be helped by Bible scholars and theologians, sometimes outside of our evangelical tradition, to loosen the straitjacket of tradition, culture and ideological influences that may limit and distort what the Bible has to say to us.

INTRODUCTION

In *Liberation Theologians Speak to Evangelicals*, Charles Ringma shows how Liberation Theologians, often viewed suspiciously by conservative and evangelical Christians, can shed light on the inadequacies of the evangelical movement in its understanding of God's love for the poor. He shows through the lens of Liberation Theology that God's love for the poor is at the heart of mission, and as such should impact all our spiritual disciplines, underpin church experimentation and animate all Christians (rather than being left to 'heroes' of the faith).

Antidote for a Poisoned Planet? by Helen Beazley draws on criticism from theologians who may only hold to the authority of the Scriptures lightly, but whose judgements allow us to re-examine whether the stewardship model fully captures the Biblical richness of the tripartite cosmos (God-Creation-Human), whether it can successfully jostle for attention against evangelical other-worldly and anti-world spirituality, and whether stewardship thinking can really radically re-orient Christians in their relationship and obligations to Creation.

Third we can get our bearings by reading the Bible transformationally. We can expect that Scriptures will throw up challenges to our current orientation and to constantly dare us to be re-converted, re-oriented, and re-directed. When we read the Scriptures expecting to be transformed, we find the Scriptures full of surprises and plot twists.

Dave Andrews provides such a plot twist with *An Evangelical Approach to Interfaith Engagement*. We have memorised the verse "Jesus is the Way," made it an article of our faith, and allowed it to be the expression of Christianity's exclusive access to God. But Dave Andrews takes that article of faith and makes it a framework for *inclusive* interfaith dialogue by exploring the 'Way' that Jesus in the Gospels advocated engaging with people from other traditions and religions. Dave then takes that framework and uses it as his framework for relating to people from other traditions and religions, giving us tips on how 'Christians' can work with 'non-Christians', suggestions for faithful multi-faith meditations and conversations, and what he calls a 'Christ-like' way we can share our faith with people of other faiths.

In *Australia - Whose Land?* Peter Adam allows himself to be utterly transformed by the Bible's clear ethical teaching which, he convincingly argues, must be applied in all its fullness to the sinfulness of Europeans towards Indigenous Australians. He discusses the unbiblical nature of European land theft, the Biblical legitimacy of Aboriginal land claims, the history of injustice against Indigenous Australians, and appropriate Christian responses.

About the writers

Peter Adam contributed *Australia - Whose Land?* Peter is the Principal of Ridley Melbourne, where he leads the College, lectures in theology, mentors students, and preaches in Chapel. Ridley College celebrated its Centenary last year (see www.ridley.edu.au). Peter trained for the ministry at Ridley, and was ordained in Melbourne. He studied in England and lectured at St John's College, Durham. He was minister of St Jude's Carlton in Melbourne for 20 years, working with university students, people in the High Rise Estates, and inner-city families. He also ran The Timothy Institute, training preachers.

Peter has written four books: *The Majestic Son: A Commentary on Hebrews; Speaking God's Words: A Practical Theology of Preaching; Hearing God's Words: Exploring, Biblical Spirituality; and Written for us: Receiving God's words in the Bible.* He edited the history of Ridley, *Proclaiming Christ: Ridley College Melbourne 1910-2010.* He has also written several booklets on spirituality and church history.

Peter has spoken at conventions and conferences for preachers in England, Scotland, New Zealand, Pakistan, and India. He enjoys reading history and fiction, playing the piano, and being walked by his dog Bella.

Dave Andrews has co-contributed *Supporting HIV Prevention as People of Faith* and contributed *An Evangelical Approach to Interfaith Engagement.* Dave and his wife Ange, and their family, have lived and worked in intentional communities with marginalised groups of people in Australia, Afghanistan, Pakistan and India for 35 years. Dave is interested in radical spirituality, incarnational community and the dynamics of personal and social transformation. Dave works as an educator at large for TEAR Australia.

He is author of many books and articles, including *Christi-Anarchy, Not Religion But Love, Building A Better World, Living Community, Compassionate Community Work and Plan Be.* Dave and Ange and their friends started Aashiana, Sahara, and Sharan – three very well-known Christian community organisations working with slum dwellers, sex workers, drug addicts, and people with HIV/AIDS in India. They are currently a part of the Waiters Union, an inner-city Brisbane Christian community network walking and working alongside Indigenous people, refugees and people with disabilities.

Helen Beazley contributed *Antidote for a Poisoned Planet?* Helen is part of the Waiters Union network in inner city Brisbane, made up of people from various walks of life, living in friendship and solidarity with people on the margins. She is a committed supporter of TEAR Australia, a faith based development organisation and sits on the TEAR Australia Board. Helen is also engaged in faith-based and community-based sustainability experiments. Helen shares her life with her husband, two daughters, and two pekin hens.

Mark Delaney contributed *Navigating the Meanings of Being a 'Christian'*. Mark grew up in Lismore on the New South Wales North Coast. He and Cathy studied at The University of Queensland in the 1980s. They married in 1993 and have lived in Delhi since 1995, returning to Brisbane for breaks every couple of years.

Mark's official role is working with Emmanuel Hospital Association, a large north Indian Christian medical NGO. Unofficially, their focus is on living in a poor Muslim neighbourhood in Delhi where they attempt to 'bring a little more of the Kingdom of God,' partly through a small advocacy project there, but also simply through relationships with friends and neighbours.

Ross Farley has contributed *Evangelism in a Pluralist Society*. His career in full time Christian ministry has included six years with Brisbane Youth for Christ in high school youth ministry, eight years as a youth pastor for a local church, and ten years with the Scripture Union of Queensland where he was responsible for coordinating training ministries and missions. Ross was also the part time chaplain for a private school.

Currently Ross is the Queensland State Coordinator for TEAR Australia. TEAR is a Christian aid and development organisation and Ross' role includes education, Bible teaching and writing resources. He is also a visiting lecturer for Christian Heritage College. Ross is author of *Strategy for Youth Leaders, Following Jesus and Leading People* and *Strategy for Youth Leaders for the 21st Century*. He is co-author of *Incite, Making a World of Difference*. Ross is a graduate of the Bible College of Queensland. His postgraduate degrees include a Graduate Diploma in Religious Education and a Master of Arts majoring in leadership studies.

Greg Manning has co-contributed *Supporting HIV Prevention as People of Faith*. Greg Manning is a bus driver, working with the Brisbane City Council. Greg and Katie and their children lived in India for 11 years between 1993 and 2007.

Greg's experience with HIV and AIDS grew with his relationships with the men in his Indian neighbourhood, who began injecting pharmaceuticals they bought in local chemists to manage the rising cost of heroin. He supported the formalisation of HIV prevention and care into programs and government policy while working with an Indian non-Government organisation called Sharan. During his last two years in India, Greg was involved with networks of people living with HIV in the South Asia region, who were struggling to make medical treatment accessible to larger populations. He also worked with populations of drug users and their service providers in India's North Eastern states to provide better access to HIV prevention services.

Charles Ringma has contributed *Liberation Theologians*

Speak to Evangelicals. Charles is an urban and cross-cultural missional worker and theologian. He is Research Professor at Asian Theological Seminary in Manila, Emeritus Professor of Mission Studies at Regent College, Vancouver, and honourary PhD supervisor at The University of Queensland, Brisbane. Among his many books are reflections on Thomas Merton, Martin Luther King Jr., Dietrich Bonhoeffer, Henri Nouwen, Mother Teresa and Jaques Ellul.

Acknowledgements

This book was originally conceived as a 'festschrift' celebrating some of the theological lessons that that some of us in the Waiters Union have learned over the last 25 years. Contributors include people who have belonged to or befriended Waiters, or have influenced and inspired many of us in Waiters in our efforts to live out the fullness of the gospel of Christ. The editors would like to thank Queensland's Uniting Church Vision for Mission Team whose funding has made work on this book possible. Thanks also to Community Initiatives Resource Association Inc. for agreeing to publish *Bearings*. Thanks to all the writers who sought no financial reward even though they brought to bear considerable expertise in their contributions, and undertook extensive research, reflection and writing.

Disclaimer

The contributors to this anthology are united in their passion to understand and apply the Scriptures with integrity. But they are not 'guilty by association'. In other words each author should not be assumed to endorse the theology promoted, or positions arrived at, by the other authors. (Nor are the views of any author necessarily shared by people involved in Waiters, Community Initiatives Resource Association or the Vision for Mission Team). That is the wonderful gift of protestantism – the freedom for each of us to study the Scriptures and to voice our convictions in the context of a respectful community of grace, and then to be tested against Scriptures by others in our community.

NAVIGATING THE MEANINGS OF BEING A 'CHRISTIAN': MY JOURNEY OF DISCOVERY

Mark Delaney

During my childhood and early adult life in Australia, and then over the last 15 years in India, I have changed my understanding considerably on the question of 'What is a Christian?' Below I outline how my understanding has changed and hopefully deepened during six distinct phases. Perhaps you can identify with one of my six phases more than the others. Whichever one you identify with, however, I hope that the story enriches and broadens your understanding of being a Christian.

1. 'A Christian is someone born into a Christian family.'

I was brought up in a relatively normal, stable Australian family, which, in those days, also meant being nominally Christian. My family was part of a mainline (Methodist) church, but we only occasionally attended, usually at Easter, Christmas and for weddings and funerals. Church for me was mostly a dull and quite meaningless affair. That forgettable experience of church was, in retrospect, partly due to my lack of openness at that point of my life, and partly due to that particular church not bothering terribly to make itself relevant to young people.

The question never really arose for me, at that juncture, as to what a Christian was. I simply assumed that *everyone* in Australia was a Christian, by virtue of having been born into a nominally Christian family. Of course that is a very different scenario from India, where there are a multitude of faiths and the majority of people are not born into Christian families. Even so, in my experience, many people here in India, especially in the **mainline** and **orthodox** churches think, like I did, that if you're born into a Christian family, then you're a Christian.

That certainly is not a criticism of mainline church goers generally. I have since found some warm, generous people in the mainline churches. Indeed one advantage of this understanding is its non-judgementalism and the acceptance it conveys to others. People holding this view tend to accept other Christians quite readily regardless of their beliefs, and accept people of other faiths since, after all, 'They're Hindus because they're born Hindus,' 'Muslim since they're born Muslim,' and so on. In a very fractious and conflictual age, this accepting, conciliatory mode of being has real advantages.

The problem with this understanding, however, is its lack of support in Scripture. On the contrary, Scripture would seem to teach against such a position. In John 8 Jesus confronts the Jews with their false view that being physiological descendants of Abraham carries any particular weight. "If you were Abraham's children," said Jesus, "then you would do the things Abraham did" (John 8:39).[1] By extension, we might assume that a 'Christian' according to Jesus, is someone who does what Jesus did!

The view also leads to a fairly passive faith, since one does not need to *do* anything to maintain it, a similar difficulty we'll see shortly, to the evangelical view.

---

[1] For this essay, Scripture is taken from the Holy Bible, NEW INTERNATIONAL VERSION®. Copyright © 1973, 1978, 1984 by Biblica, Inc. All rights reserved worldwide. Used by permission.

Then, during my teens, my mainline view was challenged for the first time when my oldest sister told me, with some conviction, that while I was a good lad, I wasn't a Christian! Here was something new! The notion that people generally, and I specifically, were not Christian just by being born in a 'Christian' family! I didn't pursue my sister's statement, fearing that if I did, it might make life more boring. I think I had the notion in my mind that people who took their Christian faith more seriously, were somehow more boring than others, not drinking, not watching movies and so on. It wasn't until college that I came to a different understanding.

2. 'A Christian is someone who "believes" in Jesus' payment for their sin.'

When I was in college, a number of my friends started calling themselves 'born again Christians' and going to a 'fellowship'. I asked, quite innocently, what they meant by the term Christian. One of my friends took me aside and shared with me a small tract titled *Knowing God Personally*, the Australian equivalent of *The Four Spiritual Laws*, a tract that is still in circulation and widely used (www.4laws.com). That tract basically stated:

Law 1: God loves each individual and wants a personal relationship with each one of us.
Law 2: We are all sinners, while God is holy and can't be around sin.
Law 3: We need someone to pay the price to God for our sin and Jesus, the only perfect one able to do so, came to pay that price.
Law 4: If we accept Jesus as 'Saviour and Lord,' then we'll be accepted by God and be his son/daughter.

After considering this for a while, I accepted these propositions and thereupon became 'born again' (a term from Jesus' interaction with Nicodemus in John 3:3). I took the decision quite seriously, started acting a little less 'worldly' and was baptised in water (according to Jesus' teaching in Matthew 28:19).

These propositions are basically the gospel as understood by the vast majority of **evangelicals** around the world today. The evangelical understanding is certainly based more on Scripture than the mainline view, most commonly on the following passages.

Law 1: "For God so loved the world that he gave his one and only Son, that whoever believes in him shall not perish but have eternal life" (John 3:16).
Law 2: "For all have sinned and fall short of the glory of God" (Romans 3:23).
"For the wages of sin is death ..." (Romans 6:23).
Law 3: "God demonstrates his love for us in this: While we were still sinners, Christ died for us" (Romans 5:8).
Law 4: "If you confess with your mouth, 'Jesus is Lord,' and believe in your heart that God raised him from the dead, you will be saved" (Romans 10:9).

This evangelical understanding, however, has some serious disadvantages. Since it is the dominant view in the Christian world today and was my own view for a number of years, I will spend some time outlining what I believe to be these difficulties.

Firstly, the evangelical view tends to absolve the adherent of the need to *do* much with her/his 'belief' in the world. The only action toward others specifically implored is that of witnessing, that is telling others of these truths. Apart from this, the main actions it promotes are reading the Bible and praying. While these actions are very important, and ones I do regularly, they are focused almost exclusively on the *vertical* dimension of faith, namely the relationship between oneself and God, rather than the *horizontal* aspect of faith – caring for others around us. In this way it is quite self-oriented, rather than other-oriented. Such a position emphasises words such as 'belief,' 'faith,' and 'acceptance' over words like 'obedience' and 'service.'

To justify this position, evangelicals point to passages such as Ephesians 2:8,9: "It is by grace you are saved, through faith ... not works so that no one can boast."

This passage, they suggest, teaches that nothing we can *do* can please God, rather it is simply our faith or belief that accesses God's grace to forgive us for our sins. So if I don't *actually* care for others, the unstated understanding is that that's OK, because I'm forgiven by His grace anyway. This is summed up beautifully by the bumper sticker "Not perfect just forgiven." It's what Dietrich Bonhoeffer famously called "cheap grace" – a very soft discipleship.

It is, however, an understanding that, while based on a selective reading of the epistles, ignores much of the gospels. Jesus, in the gospels, taught unequivocally the nexus between faith and action to our neighbours in saying, for example:

> Love the Lord your God with all your heart and with all your soul and with all your mind. This is the first and greatest commandment. And the second is like it, love your neighbour as yourself (Matthew 22:37, 38).

> Not everyone who says to me, 'Lord, Lord,' will enter the kingdom of heaven, but only he who does the will of my Father who is in heaven (Matthew 7:21).

> If you love me, you will obey what I command (John 15:14).

If we are to take these teachings seriously, then we might suggest that a more accurate understanding of salvation than Luther's *sola fida* (grace alone) is, 'God's grace is unmerited, but not unconditional,' the condition being to obey Jesus' command to love our neighbour. An analogy might be that a child's place in a family relies in one sense entirely on the 'grace' of the parents to bring that child into being, but her/his place in the family is conditional on treating others in the family reasonably. If a child treats other members of the family too badly, with for example violence, then he/she might need to leave the family for some time or permanently.

A second difficulty with the standard evangelical view rises from the first. The emphasis on belief over and above action in the world has provided a justification through the ages for violence in the name of God. The Crusades from 1000 on, the Inquisitions in the 1200s and forced conversion during colonial expansion from the 1600s were all perpetrated in order to force 'unbelievers' to 'believe' the right doctrine, in complete contradiction to Jesus' calls in the gospels to "love your enemies" (Matthew 5:44), be "peacemakers" (Matthew 5:9) and not be violent (Matthew 26:52).

A third disadvantage of the evangelical understanding is its reliance on an essentially violent and unjust view of the atonement, that is that God accepted the gruesome death of an entirely innocent one as payment for the misdeeds of others. This *substitutionary theory* of the atonement, while the only one taught in evangelical circles today, is in fact only one of several theories arguable from Scripture and wasn't even in circulation until Anselm in the 11th century. Prior to Anselm, the church basically understood Jesus atoning death to be a price paid, not to God, who didn't require such a payment, but rather to the devil, a view probably more in accordance with the ransom imagery used by Jesus himself in Mark 10:45: "For even the Son of Man did not come to be served, but to serve, and to give his life as a ransom for many."

Ransoms, after all, are always paid to the bad guy who took the hostage, rather than the 'good guy'. Other understandings of the atonement include the moral influence theory, Aulen's *Christus Victor* and the Anabaptist's non-violent theories.

A final disadvantage with the evangelical view comes from its quite narrow range of actions seen as 'sinful'. The classic proscribed sins were personal holiness matters like drinking, smoking, and sexual fidelity. While personally believing these things to indeed be poor behaviour, I've come to see other actions such as greed, over-consumption, disregard for the poor, revenge taking, and blatant exploitation of the earth's resources as equally 'sinful'. The evangelical right in the US has more recently redefined the only two sins that matter as being abortion and homosexuality. Any president, therefore, who promotes (or at least does not vehemently oppose) them is seen as 'liberal' and any president that does oppose them is seen as Godly, regardless of his other actions. Lying, fraud, deliberate disregard for the poor, overthrow of democratically elected regimes, assassinations and so on are all forgiven if he opposes abortion and homosexuality, interestingly two actions about which Christ himself said virtually nothing!

This is of course a generalisation. Many evangelicals do practise social justice with a passion, but by and large the majority of folk who take the label evangelical do suffer the disadvantages mentioned above. Even then, this is not so much a criticism of evangelicals generally, many of whom are my close friends and genuine, loving people. Rather it is a criticism of a false understanding that's been perpetrated within evangelicalism ever since the Reformation's (correct) reaction to an over emphasis on *works* in the institutional Catholic church of the day. And like most of us, evangelicals tend to believe what they're *taught* to believe, rather than reading Scripture independently and deciding for themselves what it is to be a Christian. Also like most of us, they tend to read Scripture in a way that allows them to go on living essentially selfish lives.

While I was struggling with all of this, some other Christian friends sent me on two more paths. One group told me that I wasn't a Christian unless I had been specifically chosen by God. Another group said that while I had been baptised with water, I still wasn't a real Christian until I was 'baptised in the Spirit'!

3. 'A Christian is someone who's been chosen by God from the start.'

Predestination, as this understanding is known, basically teaches that God has chosen (or predestined) from the beginning of time just who will and who will not be with Him in heaven. The teaching is based primarily on a passage in Romans 9.

Therefore God has mercy on whom he wants to have mercy, and he hardens whom he wants to harden (Romans 9:18).

Does not the potter have the right to make out of the same lump of clay some pottery for noble purposes and some for common use? (Romans 9:21).

What if God, choosing to show his wrath and make his power known, bore with great patience the objects of his wrath – prepared for destruction? What if he did this to make the riches of his glory known to the objects of his mercy, whom he prepared in advance for glory (Romans 9:22,23).

Further, I was told, the number of those already chosen by God has been fixed at 144,000 (based on Revelation 14:1). It is the position taken by some groups of Christians particularly the **Calvinist/Reformed/Presbyterian** church and some sects, most notably the Mormons.

When I heard this proposition I was astounded. I had come to believe that God was incredibly loving, based on His revelation of himself to us in Jesus, the most loving, self-sacrificial person to ever have lived. I therefore couldn't believe that a loving God would deliberately create some people just to send them to destruction. It made us out to be puppets in a cosmic play, directed by forces beyond ourselves. Hindu friends may well accept the proposition more readily, similar as it is to the notion of karma or destiny, but to me the idea of predestination seemed, and still seems, monstrous.

In its defence, some Presbyterians have come to hold the predestination view more lightly, concentrating instead on the mystery of God's ways. They point out, as does in fact Paul himself, that we need to realise that we are not God and do not know everything. Paul's retort is also for me: "Who are you oh Man, to talk back to God?" (Romans 9:20).

Nonetheless, I certainly hope God is, in reality, more like Jesus' picture of a good father than predestination's view of God as a puppeteer!

4. 'A Christian is someone who practises the gifts of the Spirit.'

Soon after I was 'born again' and baptised at college, some Charismatic/Pentecostal friends told me that there was, in fact, a 'second' baptism, a baptism of God's Spirit, through which I could access the multitude of God's wonderful gifts of the Spirit. These friends pointed to passages like:

> And these signs will accompany those who believe: they will drive out demons in my name; they will speak in new tongues … (Mark 16:17).
>
> The Holy Spirit came on them, and they spoke in tongues and prophesied (Acts 19:6).

These verses showed, they said, that I needed to be 'baptised in the Spirit' and speak in tongues in order to be a real Christian. After such a baptism, they suggested, my worship would be richer, my heart warmer, my spirit more open, and my gifts more useful. That sounded good to me, so I allowed them to pray for me. I did in fact receive the gift of speaking in another tongue, a gift which I still gladly use occasionally to communicate with God when English (or Hindi) won't do.

This position, that a real Christian will practise the gifts of the Spirit as listed in say 1 Corinthians 12, is still held by many **Charismatic** and **Pentecostal** folk. As with the evangelical understanding of a 'Christian,' there is some support in the Scriptures.

As with the evangelical position however, there are pitfalls. In looking at Scripture myself, I found the use of tongues seemed primarily to be intended for the benefit of the speaker, rather than for others. Looking more closely at 1 Corinthians 14 (especially v28), I came to see that Paul had similar misgivings, summarised in that famous wedding passage in 1 Corinthians 13: "If I speak in tongues of men and angels, but have not love, I am only a resounding gong or a clanging cymbal."

Here and in many other passages in the gospels (e.g. Matthew 22:37,38; John 13:34), the greatest result of the Spirit seemed to be the ability, not to speak in tongues, or to heal but to *love*. At this juncture I think it's important, given the media's hijacking of the term love (as lust), to reaffirm the Biblical notion of love as the sacrificial giving of one's self for others.

Again I'd hasten to recognise that these descriptions of Presbyterians and Pentecostals are of course generalisations and that many in these groups do, in fact, love their neighbour better than I.

So after four different understandings of what it meant to be a Christian, none of which sat very well with me, I was still searching, when my friend from college invited me to that destination of many spiritual searches – India! It was here that I found an understanding that finally made sense – the notion of 'following Christ' on the path of self-sacrificial love.

5. 'A Christian is someone who "follows" Jesus in practising self-sacrificial love.'

When I came to India in 1989, I came face to face with real poverty for the first time. In Australia, poverty is present, but on a much smaller scale and the Government/NGO services to help the poor are much better resourced. In India, however, poverty was everywhere. In fact, it was the bitter experience of the majority of people!

It was one particular experience with a poor man, that changed my view of being a Christian – indeed it changed my life. I remember distinctly meeting the man in a small slum in a north Indian city. With my limited Hindi, I understood him to say that he lived in this 'home,' in front of which we stood on that cold winter morning. The 'home' was no more than a tent made of plastic and timber. It was December and very cold. When I shook hands with him, his hand felt like a block of ice. Added to this, he told me that his wife had just a few days earlier given birth to their second baby, right there in that hut, presumably with no medical assistance at all.

It was a simple interaction but it shook me to the core. My evangelical training told me that this (presumably Hindu) man was a sinner and, not having accepted Christ, was going to hell. I needed to give him the 'gospel' so that he'd believe and be saved. My Charismatic training said I should pray in faith for a better house for him and his wife. Perhaps Presbyterians may have said that he wasn't one of the 'chosen.'

My *conscience*, on the other hand, said something different. My humanity suggested that this world, this system, this society, that put this man and his wife here in this freezing tent, while I had a luxurious life in Australia, was incredibly unfair and that our loving God must be very unhappy about it. My conscience said that I should be helping this man in his poverty, before I attempted to communicate about Christ, or pray for him, or do anything else.

So I attempted to help that man and his wife and in a way, that simple interaction set me on the journey to spend 15 years of my life attempting to help others like him in urban poor slums in India.

Meanwhile, I looked at the Scriptures again and found, to my relief, that the gospels were in fact, full of references to justice and God's heart for the poor! Particularly striking was the parable of Lazarus in Luke 16:19ff. Here was a poor man, much like the one I'd met, taken to heaven, with no reference to his *belief* at all. It appeared he was there in heaven, simply *because* he was poor in this life. By contrast, the rich man, someone much like me, was in hell, not because of his disbelief or lack of faith but, it appeared, simply by virtue of his ignoring poor Lazarus when he had the resources to help. If this were true then the opposite of what I'd been taught was the case; I the rich Christian was going to hell, while this man, the poor Hindu, was going to heaven! Luke's version of the beatitudes only added fuel to the fire: "Woe to you who are rich (well fed, laugh), for you will mourn and weep" (Luke 6:23ff).

As did Jesus' remarks after dealing with the rich young man.

> How hard it is for the rich to enter the kingdom of God (Mark 10:23).

> But many who are first will be last, and the last first (Mark 10:31).

I don't now believe this is the whole truth regarding wealth, but it was certainly enough to destabilise me at the time, to start me questioning what I'd been taught in my evangelical upbringing *and* to reassure me that God was very interested in the state of the world, in justice and in my response to it.

I also found in Scripture many references to God's expectation that we get personally involved in caring for people physically and emotionally as well as spiritually. Disturbingly, I found that if we don't we won't go to heaven, regardless it seemed of what we *believed*. For example, I found passages like:

> But if you do not forgive men their sins, your Father will not forgive your sins (Matthew 6:15).

> I tell you the truth, whatever you did not do [feeding the hungry, inviting the stranger in, clothing the naked, visiting the prisoner] for one of the least of these, you did not do for me. Then they will go away to eternal punishment (Matthew 25:45,46).

> Those who have done good will rise to live, and those who have done evil will rise to be condemned (John 5:29).

This notion of our faith requiring us to actually *do* something about situations of need/injustice, raised another challenge to my evangelical heritage. It suggested that *works* or what I actually *do* to and for others, had a strong impact on whether I was saved or not. And this was in direct contradiction, so it seemed, to the much quoted Ephesians 2 passage cited earlier.

I don't still believe that these verses are actually contradictory, but only appear so, because of too narrow an understanding of the words *faith* and *belief* in passages like John 3:16, John 5:24, Romans 10:9, Ephesians 2:8 and so on. I am now able to reconcile these seemingly conflicting passages by the notion of 'following Christ' on the journey of self-sacrificial love.

I found that Jesus himself often talked about following him as the key to salvation. His invitation to Matthew was *"Follow me"* (Matthew 9:9) and his challenge to the same Matthew along with the other disciples several years later was: "if anyone would come after me, he must deny himself and take up his cross and follow me" (Matthew 16:24).

Following is I think based on *belief*, since one normally *believes* someone before *following* her/him, but *following* further implies putting that faith/belief into action. A story I have heard about the tight rope walker Blondin has helped me see the connection. According to the story, after one of Blondin's famous tightrope walks across Niagara Falls in front of a large delighted crowd, he said to the crowd, "Do you *believe* that I can walk back across the rope pushing a wheelbarrow?" "Yes!" enthused the crowd, eager to see an even more daring feat. "Then if you believe," challenged Blondin, "get in the wheelbarrow!" The story shows better than any other I know that belief, real belief, requires action.

Following Christ in self-sacrificial love has historically been the great gift of the **Catholics**. Francis of Assisi, St Ignatius and more recently Mother Theresa have all been magnificent in their following of Christ in sacrificially caring for the least. Certainly in Catholicism there have been excesses and poor teaching. Many Catholics have given up an active following of Christ's footsteps to instead follow a set of traditions. Before this too, the medieval Catholic church had been grossly guilty of false doctrine, teaching that giving money to the church would, in effect, pay God back for their sin in a kind of spiritual bank account – the infamous indulgences. It was one of the main errors against which Luther rightly railed. Unfortunately, however, a valid protest against the abuse of power by the institutional Catholic church, led ultimately to the protestant devaluing of works/action altogether.

The notion of *following* is very useful in calling us to put our faith into action. One disadvantage to the view, however, is that it is still a little passive in its nature, carrying as it does the sense that we wait to be told what to do by the one we follow. The following view also tends to focus on sacrificial care in a relatively narrow range of issues, namely poverty, hunger, the homeless, orphans and so on.

Once back in Australia after my emotional and theological turmoil in India I completed my Law degree and practised as an apprentice lawyer for a while. I had, however, a new sense of purpose in life, to follow Jesus in helping to care for the marginalised in the forgotten parts of the world. After marrying in 1993, my wife Cathy and I returned to India in 1995 to follow Christ to one of the hard places, the slums of Delhi. We moved into a poor neighbourhood, lived simply beside our poor neighbours and sought to hear how Christ would have us serve. Over the years since, that *following* has meant a variety of things in a variety of contexts, from helping a widow to get a pension, to assisting a heart patient to get surgery, to sharing our faith in Christ with friends who ultimately came to follow Him.

Over the years in India we have found one more (although probably not the last) idea of what it means to be a Christian to be very helpful, that of 'the Kingdom of God.'

6. 'A Christian is one who partners with God in helping His Kingdom to come.'

It seems to me from the gospels that God's ultimate desire in dealing with us is to bring His Kingdom on earth. This is clearly seen in the most famous of Jesus' prayers: "Your kingdom come, Your will be done, on earth as it is in Heaven" (Matthew 6:10).

The *Kingdom* also featured in Jesus' first public appearance when he said, "The time has come. The kingdom of God is near. Repent and believe the good news" (Mark 1:15).

The *Kingdom* was also important enough for Jesus that he begins many of his parables with *"the Kingdom of heaven is like ... "* (e.g. Mark 4:26; 4:30).

So what is this Kingdom and what does it mean for us in our discipleship? Never having lived under a king, we find it difficult to understand. Indeed most kings and queens we know of have abused their power and overseen exploitative Kingdoms.

Many Christians interpret the Kingdom to be a state that will never occur in this age, only an ideal that will come about in the next life. However, by saying "on earth as it is in heaven" Jesus himself seems to indicate that the Kingdom is in fact possible on this earth, at least to some degree!

Jesus defines the Kingdom in the Lord's Prayer as "your will be done." He also unpacks the Kingdom early in his ministry in the synagogue at Nazareth, when he says that he has been anointed "to preach the good news to the poor." He follows this immediately by describing what this good news is, saying, "He has sent me to proclaim freedom for the prisoners and recovery of sight for the blind, to release the oppressed, to proclaim the year of the Lord's favour" (Luke 4:18ff).

Thus it is likely that the *good news* being preached to the poor was that God's Kingdom – a society in which those at the bottom of human society are cared for and valued – was on its way into our world! Unfortunately, this good news of the Kingdom to the poor seems to be quite 'bad news' to the well off in this society – as evidenced by the parable of Lazarus and the rich man discussed previously and Luke's "woes" to the rich and well fed (Luke 6:24ff).

This Kingdom then, being a reversal of the current order, so that the poor and marginalised are exalted and cared for also now makes perfect sense of Jesus' strange statement, "the last shall be first and the first last" (Mark 10:31), and of Mary's Magnificat in prophesying on the effect of Jesus coming: "He has brought down the rulers from their thrones, but has lifted up the humble. He has filled the hungry with good things but has sent the rich away empty" (Luke 2:52,53).

It also explains Jesus' constant urging to care for the poor, the strangers, the prisoners and so on (Matthew 25:31ff; Matthew 5:1-10; Luke 14:12-14) as this is what is necessary for the coming of God's Kingdom on earth. The prophets too are full of this notion – God urging his people to work with Him to create this just and equitable society: "What oh man does the Lord require of you? but to do justice and love mercy and walk humbly with your God" (Micah 6:8).

Deciding what the Kingdom of God looks like on earth is sometimes obvious, as with the abomination of world poverty, human trafficking and the like. It sometimes, however, requires considerable wisdom and thought and it is in this that it is a more interactive, collaborative notion than simply *following*.

Recently, for example, Christians have realised that helping to bring the Kingdom also includes caring for the environment, peacemaking, human rights, and challenging our own overconsumption; areas traditionally avoided as too 'secular' by other streams of the church.

A final advantage to this Kingdom view is its taking Jesus' teaching, especially in the Sermon on the Mount, as serious propositions to be put into practice, rather than ideals to be preached about, but never seriously sought.

This Kingdom work is perhaps best seen in history by the **Anabaptists** including the Mennonites, Brethren and various Christian peace communities around the world. They focus their attention on living out their faith in an attempt to partner with God in seeing, even if in a small way, his Kingdom come in their area. Some, like the Amish, have attempted to create quite exclusive communities in which they can recreate the Kingdom, by excluding the 'evil world'. Most, however, recognise that Christ called us to be salt and light (Matthew 5:13ff) in our Kingdom building activities, so positively affecting the evil world, rather than insulating ourselves from it.

The Kingdom view is often criticised, especially by evangelicals, as not being essentially different from secular social concern for the poor. To this I would suggest that any action that cares for the poor is in fact, a Godly action, whether or not it is recognised as such by the doer, since, "Whatever you did for the least of these brothers of mine, you did for me" (Matthew 25:40).

I'd also suggest that for someone to do this 'secular social work' over the long haul, one actually needs a firm spiritual base. Otherwise once the money runs out most professional social workers will leave, having done their couple of years of good for the world.

This then is my current understanding of our role, to partner humbly with God in building His Kingdom on earth. It is the vision that keeps us in the slums of Delhi. I wouldn't claim that we have seen a rapid expansion of the Kingdom in the communities in which we have lived, but I would like to think that we have sown a number of seeds, where perhaps the Kingdom may grow.

Holding the good from all

While I feel my understanding of what it means to be a Christian has changed for the good over the years, I recognise that I don't have all truth, that I may well be wrong and may change my view further in the coming years.

It is also important for me, and for us all, to appreciate the good in every stream of faith. Thus it is important that I still hold on to the inclusiveness of my mainstream church upbringing, the zealous desire to share my faith with others from my evangelical season and the Pentecostal ability to bring healing through the Spirit of God. So too do I need to hold onto the reverence for God's sovereignty championed by the Presbyterians, the tireless action of following Christ in selfless care for the marginalised of the Catholics and the creative, peaceful, Kingdom building initiatives of the Anabaptists.

We might summarise these six understandings in the table below.

A Christian is one who ...	Emphasised Scripture Key verses	Positives	Pitfalls	Representative Denomination
1. ... is born a Christian.	?	*Acceptance of others *Stability	*Passivity *Lack of basis in Scripture	*Mainline *Orthodox
2. ... believes Jesus died for their sins.	Epistles "if you confess with your mouth 'Jesus is Lord,' and believe in your heart that God raised him from the dead, you will be saved" (Romans 10:9). "It is by grace you are saved, through faith ... not works so that no one can boast" (Ephesians 2:8,9).	*Concern for correct doctrine *Biblical basis *Willingness to witness *Emphasis on grace *Purity of character	*De-emphasises action *Emphasises epistles over the gospels *Relies on unjust view of atonement *Uncritical belief of what taught *Narrow list of what is 'sinful'	*Evangelical *Independent

A Christian is one who ...	Emphasised Scripture Key verses	Positives	Pitfalls	Representative Denomination
3. ... is one of God's predetermined chosen.	Romans "Therefore God has mercy on whom he wants to have mercy, and he hardens whom he wants to harden" (Romans 9:18).	*Submission to God *Space for mystery	*Passive *Exclusive *Narrow scriptural base	*Reformed *Presbyterian
4. ... is baptised in the Spirit and manifests the gifts.	Acts "the Holy Spirit came on them, and they spoke in tongues and prophesied" (Acts 19:6).	*Heartfelt worship *Openness to the spiritual realm *Faith God will act *Use of spiritual gifts (e.g. healing) for the good of others	*Emotions over logic *Prioritising some gifts over greater gift of love	*Charismatic *Pentecostal
5. ... follows Jesus in selfless care for the poor.	Gospels "I tell you the truth, whatever you did not do for one of the least of these, you did not do for me" (Matthew 25:45,46).	*Obedience *Serving the poor *Going to hard places *Powerful witness in a broken world	*Reliance on tradition *Blind following of leadership *Relatively narrow poverty focus	*Catholic
6. ... helps God build His kingdom.	Sermon on the mount "Your Kingdom come, Your will be done, on earth as it is in Heaven" (Matthew 6:10).	*Wholistic and creative (environmental, peace-building etc) *Community focus *Based on Jesus' main body of teaching	*Tendency to exclusive communities *Indistinguish-able from secular social work	*Mennonite *Christian peace communities

Holding together the good in each stream is beautifully seen in the society founded by the early believers, described in Acts 2. Most of the positive sides of each of the six streams I have described are present there.

> They devoted themselves to the apostles' teaching and to the fellowship, to the breaking of bread and to prayer. Everyone was filled with awe, and many wonders and miraculous signs were done by the apostles. All the believers were together and had everything in common. Selling their possessions and goods, they gave to anyone as he had need. Every day they continued to meet together in the temple courts. They broke bread in their homes and ate together with glad and sincere hearts, praising God and enjoying the favour of all the people and the Lord added to their number daily those who were being saved (Acts 2:42-47).

What a wonderful picture of the Kingdom of God here on earth. And what a beautiful picture of what it means to be a Christian. May we have the courage to be like those early Christians, and all the more courage since it is, for many of us, so different from our current expression of faith.

EVANGELISM IN A PLURALIST SOCIETY: LESSONS FROM NEW TESTAMENT EVANGELISM

Ross Farley

Paul commanded Timothy to "do the work of an evangelist" (2 Timothy 4:5).[1] While many Christians have fairly firm ideas about what is entailed in evangelism, the New Testament teaching on this subject raises a number of questions about current evangelical practices.

Much of what gets called 'evangelism' is not really evangelism at all and is often just programs to entertain Christians. Non-Christians are supposed to come but they don't, so Christians get together and enjoy themselves and call it all 'evangelism'. If non-Christians attend at all, they are vastly outnumbered in Christian-controlled contexts where Christians maintain the power position. When real evangelism occurs, it is often not even recognised as evangelism. Real evangelism is usually out there in the world of non-Christians where other Christians can't see what is going on. It occurs in non-Christian contexts, where Christians are outnumbered and don't have the luxury of the power position. That is what happened in New Testament evangelism. Christians did not organise evangelistic activities to which non-Christians were invited. Evangelism occurred when Christians went to the synagogues, market-places, courts and other places controlled by non-Christians. Contemporary evangelism is often on our turf and under our terms while New

---

[1] For this essay, Scripture taken from the Holy Bible, NEW INTERNATIONAL VERSION®. Copyright © 1973, 1978, 1984 by Biblica, Inc. All rights reserved worldwide. Used by permission.

Testament evangelism was on their turf, where non-Christians often had considerable power. Consequently New Testament evangelism involved considerable risk. The book of Acts recounts that those who engaged in evangelism were not cheered and clapped but beaten, stoned, imprisoned, killed or run out of town.

A large range of practices are labeled 'evangelism' and some of them have little in common with the approaches of Jesus and the apostles. Evangelism is a big topic about which much could be written however, allow me to make three observations about evangelism in the New Testament that have contemporary relevance.

1. New Testament evangelism called for repentance and faith, not the sinner's prayer and decisions.

The goal of much contemporary evangelism is for people to make a 'decision' for Christ and to pray a prayer of acceptance, often called a sinner's prayer. In contrast, Jesus and the apostles called people to repent and believe. Now many people who make a decision and pray the prayer may well be repenting and believing, but it is often presented in a way that is quite disconnected from faith and repentance. Reducing conversion to a formula is quite foreign to New Testament evangelism. Nowhere in the New Testament is anyone ever asked to pray the sinner's prayer and nowhere in the New Testament does a Christian ever say to a non-Christian that Jesus died for your sins. The atonement was taught in the New Testament to believers (in places like Romans), but never to unbelievers as part of the evangelistic process.[2] (Check out the evangelistic sermons in Acts.)

These two facts alone demolish so much of the 'gospel message' that many Christians believe should be presented to non-Christians. This message goes like this: "Jesus died for your sins. You need to accept his death on your behalf. You do this by making a decision or praying the sinner's prayer." No one in the New Testament approached evangelism in that sort of a way. This approach is a construction of evangelicalism, not an approach learnt from Jesus and the apostles. (It is, of course, true that Jesus died for our sins, but this was not preached to unbelievers in the New Testament.)

Instead of decisions and the sinner's prayer, Jesus and the apostles called for faith and repentance. Their focus was on the Kingdom of God. The King has come and we must submit to his rule and that starts with faith and repentance. When they preached, they often used the word 'repent' and the teaching of Jesus made clear what type of life changes Jesus was looking for. Some of Jesus' personal encounters are very enlightening, he really helped people come to terms with what faith and repentance would mean in their lives. On two occasions Jesus was asked, "What must I do to inherit eternal life?" He did not respond with the standard evangelical answers, ask them to

---

[2] The death of Jesus was sometimes referred to in New Testament preaching but it was not used to teach the atonement. The apostles referred to the crucifixion of Jesus especially when preaching to Jews, but they did not use the suffering of Jesus to teach that Jesus died for our sins. They used it to prove that Jesus was the Messiah as he fitted the Old Testament expectations that the Messiah would suffer. Acts 17:2-4 makes that point: Jesus had to suffer to be the Messiah that the Old Testament predicted. The apostles did teach substitutionary atonement to people who already had responded to the message preached in Acts. Therefore it is in the epistles that references to the atonement as a central part of the gospel can be found. The atonement explains how salvation works, but it is not necessary for people to understand that in order to be converted or else the Acts sermons would need to be very different. I am not saying that we must never teach the atonement to unbelievers. The more they know about what the Bible teaches the better. However it is very harmful to teach the atonement instead of calling people to repentance.

make a decision or pray a prayer. How then did Jesus respond when asked about the way of salvation?

- One of these occasions was the story of the rich young man (Mark 10:17-27). Jesus led the young man to reflect on the Old Testament law and then told him to sell his posessions and give to the poor. In doing so he challenged him to cast down his false gods (his possessions), so that he could put his faith in the true God. Jesus also defined repentance for this man. He had to repent of his covetous and materialistic lifestyle and he could no longer see people in need and do nothing.

- On the other occasion (Luke 10:25-37) the question was asked by an expert in the law. Once again Jesus led the man to reflect on the Old Testament law and the man then asked, "Who is my neighbour?" In reply, Jesus told the story of the Good Samaritan which demonstrated what it means to be a neighbour. Jesus concluded the story with "go and do likewise," spelling out what repentance would mean for that man.

In both these stories, when Jesus was asked about the way of salvation, he did not resort to evangelical formulas but led each man to understand what faith and repentance would mean for them. 'Repentance' and 'faith' were not presented as theological abstractions, but these men were left in no doubt as to what it would mean for them to submit to the rule of God in their lives. Their lifestyles were measured against God's standards and they were faced with choices that related to real life. There were no prayers, no esoteric religious experiences, just the call to faith and repentance. It seems that the rich young man rejected

Jesus' offer but Zacchaeus (Luke 19:1-10) made an immediate and dramatic response to Jesus with a complete change of lifestyle, demonstrating true faith and repentance. Once again there was no sinner's prayer but Jesus announced, "Today salvation has come to this house." This was real conversion, where people counted the cost before becoming followers of Jesus. While Jesus upheld the hope of eternal life, he did not seek to entice the unwilling.

Now imagine that Jesus is living today in our communities and he dealt with people like he dealt with the men in these gospel stories. Let's suppose that Jesus challenged them about their attitudes to their possessions and the false sense of security they bring. Let's suppose he helped them explore their materialistic values, unjust behaviours and their lack of compassion for others. What would happen? I reckon that some would probably repent while others would dislike Jesus, but few would dismiss it all as irrelevant mumbo-jumbo as Christian evangelism is so often dismissed today.

Repentance and faith involves facing up to real life, not ritualistic prayers and religious procedures. In contemporary evangelism the word 'sin' is often used as an abstract, theological concept and unbelievers often think sin refers to the things in their lives that are fun and enjoyable. Jesus usually did not talk about sin as a theological abstraction, but as behaviour and attitudes that are clearly seen to be ugly and harmful. People are often converted, not when we talk in theological abstractions, but when we put the finger right on the problem in their lives.

People cannot earn salvation through doing good works and they need to hear of God's offer of forgiveness. However while salvation is unmerited, it is not unconditional but requires the response of faith and repentance. We are most helpful to unbelievers when we help them to identify how God wants their lives to change (repent)[3] and to cast down the false gods in their lives so they can trust the true God (believe).

I have heard many 'gospel messages' where the concepts of faith and repentance, so central to New Testament preaching, are completely absent. Bank robbers could hear the message and believe that they could gain eternal life and continue robbing banks.

2. New Testament evangelism was holistic, not dualistic.

Let's start by clarifying terms. A *dualistic* approach divides life into two spheres, the spiritual and the physical. Spiritual aspects of life like prayer, church and Bible reading are seen as good and God is involved in this area of life. On the other hand, physical aspects of life are seen as evil or at least, not what God really cares about. Dualism comes from non-Christian sources like the ancient Greek philosophers. It is not a Biblical worldview and some sections of the New Testament are even written to refute dualism. Nevertheless many Christians (often unconsciously) embrace a dualistic worldview. This leads them to think that Christian service can only consist of spiritual activities like preaching, praying and going to church. On the other hand, addressing physical or social needs (e.g. homelessness, poverty, self-harm) cannot be considered as genuine Christian service because God is less interested in these physical aspects of life. Although dualism is contrary to Biblical teaching,

---

[3] I am not suggesting that everyone can totally change in an instant. Repentance is often a slow process but there must be a turn-around in people's lives.

dualistic Christians tend to edit the Scriptures and filter out the passages that call for physical and social needs to be addressed with justice and compassion.

A *holistic* approach sees all of life as important and God is concerned with every aspect of human life: physical, mental, social and spiritual. God wants people to experience forgiveness from sin, but he also wants their social and physical needs to be met. A holistic approach to ministry means having a genuine concern for all of the needs of human beings. This does not mean their social and physical needs should be an entry point for evangelism, but that spiritual, physical and social needs are equally important.

The New Testament rejects dualism and upholds holistic models of ministry. Jesus was obviously concerned for both physical and spiritual needs. He addressed spiritual needs through preaching, teaching and casting out demons. He addressed physical needs by healing the sick and feeding the hungry, and he addressed social needs through his teaching and in the community dynamics of his own disciples. Sometimes Jesus healed people who were listening to him teach, but at other times he healed people who did not respond or even listen to his teaching. Jesus healed the servant of the high priest whose ear was severed during Jesus' arrest (Luke 22:51). On another occasion he healed ten lepers and only one returned to thank him. The other nine heard no teaching or expressed no thanks (Luke 17:11-19). It seems that Jesus healed people because they were sick and he fed people because they were hungry. Sometimes these miracles led to opportunities to teach people about spiritual things, sometimes they were even 'signs' that pointed to spiritual realities, yet Jesus also at times healed the sick and disabled without it being linked to any spiritual teaching. Sometimes Jesus addressed both physical and spiritual needs together, yet at other times he addressed spiritual needs without the physical or physical needs without the spiritual.

It is also consistent with the teaching of Jesus to respond to the physical or social needs of people whether or not there is an opportunity for evangelism. The Samaritan in the parable of *The Good Samaritan* did not weigh up the opportunities for evangelism before he helped the injured man and he is presented as an example for us (Luke 10:25-37). The fate of the rich man in the parable of *The Rich Man and Lazarus* is somehow linked to his consistent failure to respond to the poverty of Lazarus (Luke 16:19-31). Concern is expressed for the hungry, thirsty, stranger, naked, sick and prisoners in the parable of *The Sheep and the Goats* (Matthew 25:31-46). Jesus taught that it is important to both preach the gospel and respond to people in need. He did not teach that we are to help those in need only when it will provide an opportunity to preach the gospel.

This holistic pattern of ministry and evangelism was continued in the early church. There was worship and teaching, and people were converted daily yet they also addressed the needs of the sick, poor and widows (Acts 1-4). The apostles like Peter and Paul had very holistic ministries and their New Testament writings contain strong teaching against dualism (Colossians, 1 John).

Christians often imagine that Jesus and the apostles spent their lives preaching the gospel. The reality of the New Testament is that, while they did preach, they addressed a host of other human needs as well (e.g. sickness, disability, demon possession, hunger, poverty, injustice, suffering, grief, death). In fact no Christian leader in the New Testament (that we have substantial information about) just preached. They all addressed a broad range of human needs.

Jesus gave us *the great commission* (Matthew 28:18-20) but before that he gave us *the great commandment* (Luke 10:27). Many Christians have somehow got the idea that, in giving us the great commission, Jesus rescinded the great commandment. They believe that the preaching of the gospel is now so important, that it should be our sole concern and we no longer need to bother about loving our neighbors. However the great commandment has never been rescinded. Indeed it provided the relational and ethical framework in which Jesus and the apostles conducted their ministries. They reached out in love and in the context of that love, declared the message of the gospel as opportunities arose.

Christians who approach evangelism from a dualistic framework often become very frustrated. They want to reach people but they are often so removed from real life that they cannot connect with people. They want to preach but don't get the opportunities. They are interested in 'souls,' not real people; the spiritual world but not the real world people live in. The physical, emotional and social needs of people will probably be seen as barriers to 'real' ministry rather than opportunities to be Christ-like.

Christians who approach evangelism from a holistic perspective are concerned for whole people. Like Jesus they respond to all human needs whether or not people listen to their preaching. Ironically these Christians are more likely to get the opportunities to share their message.

Christians who live in countries where evangelism is illegal are often more effective at evangelism than Christians in the West. In these places, where evangelism is punishable by death or imprisonment, opportunities arise and people come to Christ. Until recently, evangelism was illegal in Nepal and carried a substantial prison sentence and yet the Nepali church grew at a much faster rate than the church in Australia where generally Christians are free to evangelise. Nepali believers reached out in love to address whatever human needs arose (e.g. food security, safe water, health care) and opportunities to meet spiritual needs also came their way. Ministry of this nature is difficult to sustain without a holistic framework. We have a lot to learn from the attitudes of Christians in countries where evangelism is banned yet the church still grows faster than in the West. The relative lack of restrictions in the West has not made us evangelistically more effective.

Holism means that we are serious about obeying both the great commandment and the great commission. If we disregard the great commandment we lose the capacity to fulfill the great commission. If we obey the great commandment, opportunities to fulfill the great commission are more likely to arise. Our main concern should be who are our neighbours? And how can we love them? Dualism generates mental barriers that cut off opportunities for mission. Holism opens up a world of opportunities and who knows where it all may lead.

3. New Testament evangelism was a two way, not a one way encounter.

There are some interesting dynamics in the story of Peter and Cornelius (Acts 10). Peter was invited to visit Cornelius (and was sent by the Holy Spirit). To cut a long story short, Cornelius and his family and friends became Christians and experienced many changes in their lives. Most evangelical Christians would expect new converts to change. However they were not the only people who changed. Peter was also changed by his encounter with Cornelius and these changes were substantial. Peter changed in the following ways.

- Peter's social mores and social boundaries changed.
- Peter's ethics changed.
- Peter's diet probably changed. (Certainly the Old Testament dietary restrictions were relaxed sometime after this.)
- Peter's religious practices and boundaries changed. (At least a process of change was begun whereby circumcision and other practices of Judaism would eventually be no longer required of believers.)
- Peter's theology changed (or at least developed further).

It was not just Peter who changed but these changes were passed on to the entire early church. Similar two way changes occurred as the story of the book of Acts progressed, so that Paul also grew and changed as he took the gospel further into Gentile territory. The Council at Jerusalem (Acts 15) and Paul's letter to the Galatians are further examples of how those who preached the gospel were themselves changed through the process of evangelism. As they faced new situations and had to come to terms with new implications of the gospel they preached, they learnt from the situations they faced and they learnt from the people who came to Christ through their message.[4] New Testament evangelism was a two way process where the converts changed but the evangelists were also changed by their encounters. The real change agent in the New Testament was not the preachers, but God who was changing people like Cornelius as well as the preachers who bore the message.

Too often Christians approach the task of evangelism as if we have it all worked out and it is only non-Christians who need to change. Sadly, evangelism is often more about attempting to make people clones of ourselves than pointing people to Christ who wants us all to become more like him. We all have a lot to learn as disciples of Jesus and a lot of changing still to do. As Peter found out, sometimes it is non-Christians or new Christians that God uses to change us to be more like Jesus.

The humility of Peter in this story is amazing. Peter was an apostle who had been personally trained by Jesus for three years. He became the leader and spokesman of the early church and he had apostolic authority so that his writings were included in the canon of Scripture. If anyone had a right to think he had it all worked out, it was Peter. Yet he was prepared to learn from Cornelius and change in ways that defied all his upbringing,

---

[4] I am not saying that Peter and the apostles received new chapters of special revelation in these events. God had revealed himself fully in Christ in the events recorded in the gospel accounts. I'm also not saying that the apostles adapted or changed the essence of the gospel message to suit new situations. I am saying that as Peter and the apostles took the gospel message into new situations, events occurred that caused them to come to new understandings of the gospel that had already been fully revealed. Through their encounters with non-Christians and new believers they came to a greater understanding of the implications of what Jesus had already done.

culture and previous religion.

Christians often approach evangelism with the attitude that we are the ones who know and that non-Christians ought to learn from us. Sometimes unbelievers are treated as if they have nothing to offer. They must learn from us but we have nothing to learn from them. Such attitudes are so contrary to the example of the apostles. We have the Bible and in it we have God's truth. However none of us fully understands that truth no matter how experienced we may be. God may have absolute truth and we may enjoy a relationship with God, but that does not mean we have absolute truth. We need to learn from the humility of Peter and be prepared to learn from anyone God brings our way. As we preach the gospel, hopefully unbelievers will learn from us but we need to also be open to learn from them.

Many people avoid Christians because some Christians think that they have all the answers and they are not prepared to listen or learn from others. Those who believe that God has revealed himself in Scripture are often regarded as somewhat dangerous: people with minds already made up because God told them, and unwilling to listen to reason or respect other people's views. There *are* Christians like that, but they have not learnt much from Peter and the other apostles. The Scriptures teach the importance of humility even (perhaps especially) when dealing with unbelievers. Christians should abandon all notions of triumphant superiority and nurture an openness to learn from everyone God brings our way.

Conclusion

No doubt the New Testament has many other important lessons to teach us about evangelism. My challenge is to read it and apply it to our situations. I conclude with this question, how would we need to change for our relationships with others who do not share our faith to be more in line with Jesus and the apostles?

AN EVANGELICAL APPROACH TO INTERFAITH ENGAGEMENT

Dave Andrews

1. The Way of Jesus

Christians often say to 'non-Christians', Jesus said, "I am the way and the truth and the life. No one comes to the Father except through me" (John 14:6).[1]

But we often neglect the Way Jesus related to people in other religious traditions, forget the Truth Jesus embodied that cannot be contained by any religion, including our own, and ignore the Life Jesus offers to all people, even 'non-Christians'.

Let's look at the very start of his ministry.

> He went to Nazareth, where he had been brought up, and on the Sabbath day he went into the synagogue as was his custom. And he stood up to read. The scroll of the prophet Isaiah was handed to him. Unrolling it, he found the place where it is written:
>
> > "The Spirit of the Lord is on me,
> > because he has anointed me
> > to preach good news to the poor.
> > He has sent me to proclaim freedom for
> > the prisoners and recovery of sight for the blind,

---

[1] In this essay Scripture taken from the Holy Bible, NEW INTERNATIONAL VERSION®. Copyright © 1973, 1978, 1984 by Biblica, Inc. All rights reserved worldwide. Used by permission.

to release the oppressed, to proclaim the year of the Lord's favor."

Then he rolled up the scroll, gave it back to the attendant and sat down. The eyes of everyone in the synagogue were fastened on him, and he began by saying to them, "Today this scripture is fulfilled in your hearing."

All spoke well of him and were amazed at the gracious words that came from his lips. "Isn't this Joseph's son?" they asked.

Jesus said to them, "Surely you will quote this proverb to me: 'Physician, heal yourself! Do here in your home town what we have heard that you did in Capernaum.'" "I tell you the truth," he continued, "no prophet is accepted in his hometown. I assure you that there were many widows in Israel in Elijah's time, when the sky was shut for three and a half years and there was a severe famine throughout the land. Yet Elijah was not sent to any of them, but to a widow in Zarephath in the region of Sidon. And there were many in Israel with leprosy in the time of Elisha the prophet, yet not one of them was cleansed – only Naaman the Syrian."

All the people in the synagogue were furious when they heard this. They got up, drove him out of the town, and took him to the brow of the hill on which the town was built, in order to throw him down the cliff. But he walked right through the crowd and went on his way (Luke 4:16-30).

Everybody was happy till he suggested that Jews, who thought they were the 'people of God,' did not have a monopoly on God. But God worked in the lives of others – even Naaman the Syrian.[2]

Jesus knew that as soon as he said that, the Jews would want to kill him, but he said it anyway.

And note the circumstance in which the prophet Elisha pronounces a blessing of peace on Naaman.

> Naaman went with his horses and chariots and stopped at the door of Elisha's house. Elisha sent a messenger to say to him, "Go, wash yourself seven times in the Jordan, and your flesh will be restored and you will be cleansed."
>
> But Naaman went away angry and said, "I thought that he would surely come out to me and stand and call on the name of the LORD his God, wave his hand over the spot and cure me of my leprosy. Are not Abana and Pharpar, the rivers of Damascus, better than any of the waters of Israel? Couldn't I wash in them and be cleansed?" So he turned and went off in a rage. Naaman's servants went to him and said, "My father, if the prophet had told you to do some great thing, would you not have done it? How much more, then, when he tells you, 'Wash and be cleansed!'"

---

[2] Brueggemann (1997, pp. 91-96) makes the following observations about non-Jewish believers: The Egyptian Pharaoh's belief was a grudging acknowledgement of Yahweh (Exodus 1-10). The homage of the Phoenician Hiram (I Kings 5:7) and the Sabaean Sheba (I Kings 10:9) was a glad acknowledgement of Yahweh. The Midianite Jethro (Exodus 18:10-11) and the Canaanite Rahab (Joshua 2:9-11) were converted to Yahweh and became Jews. Whereas the Babylonian Nebuchadnezzar (Daniel 3:28-29) and the Syrian Naaman (2 Kings 5:5) were transformed but stayed Gentiles.

So he went down and dipped himself in the Jordan seven times, as the man of God had told him, and his flesh was restored and became clean like that of a young boy. Then Naaman and all his attendants went back to the man of God. He stood before him and said, "Now I know that there is no God in all the world except in Israel. Please accept now a gift from your servant."

The prophet answered, "As surely as the LORD lives, whom I serve, I will not accept a thing." And even though Naaman urged him, he refused.

"If you will not," said Naaman, "please let me, your servant, be given as much earth as a pair of mules can carry, for your servant will never again make burnt offerings and sacrifices to any other god but the LORD. But may the LORD forgive your servant for this one thing: When my master enters the temple of Rimmon to bow down and he is leaning on my arm and I bow there also – when I bow down in the temple of Rimmon, may the LORD forgive your servant for this."

"Go in peace," Elisha said (2 Kings 5:9-19).

When people *from a group in Jesus' own tradition* criticised Jesus, he said to them, "He who is not with me is against me" (Matthew 12:30). But when his disciples criticised people who were *not in their group*, for doing Christ-like things Jesus said, "Whoever is not against us is for us" (Mark 9:40). In fact, Jesus told his disciples that not all his people are part of their group.

> I am the good shepherd; I know my sheep and my sheep know me – just as the Father knows me and I know the Father – and I lay down my life for the sheep. I have other sheep that are not of this sheep pen. I must bring them also. They too will listen to my voice, and there shall be one flock and one shepherd (John 10:16).

Jesus is clearly saying these "other sheep are not of this sheepfold" but they are still his sheep. He says, "I know my sheep and my sheep know me" – they are already familiar with his voice, so when he calls, he says, "they too will listen." After all, he says, he is their shepherd.

Given the fact that all of us know these Scriptures you would think that we would always be aware of the possibility that other people in other traditions may have a relationship with God. But I would like to suggest that Christians in general and Christian missionaries in particular, may not see other people from other traditions as being able to have a relationship with God because *we may be blinded by what I would refer to as a self-centred Christian theology.*

Let me explain what I mean. There are two major texts in Matthew's gospel from which we Christians draw our theology of mission. The first major text is in Matthew 28:18-20.

> Then Jesus came to them and said, "All authority in heaven and on earth has been given to me. Therefore go and make disciples of all nations, baptizing them in the name of the Father and of the Son and of the Holy Spirit, and teaching them to obey everything I have commanded you. And surely I am with you always, to the very end of the age."

Question: Where would you locate Jesus in this theology: with us or with them?
Answer: With us.

See the diagram below.

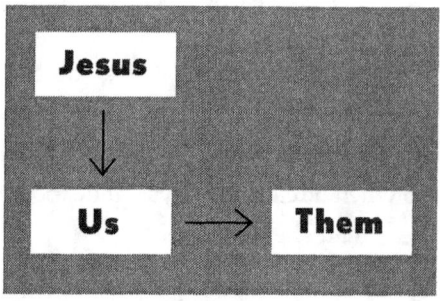

The second major text is in Matthew 25:34-40.

> Then the King will say, "Come, you who are blessed by my Father; take your inheritance, the kingdom prepared for you since the creation of the world. For I was hungry and you gave me something to eat, I was thirsty and you gave me something to drink, I was a stranger and you invited me in, I needed clothes and you clothed me, I was sick and you looked after me, I was in prison and you came to visit me." Then the righteous will answer him, "Lord, when did we see you hungry and feed you, or thirsty and give you something to drink? When did we see you a stranger and invite you in, or needing clothes and clothe you? When did we see you sick or in prison and go to visit you?" The King will reply, "I tell you the truth, whatever you did for one of the least of these brothers [and sisters] of mine, you did for me."

Question: Where would you locate Jesus in this theology: with us or with them?
Answer: With them.

See the diagram below.

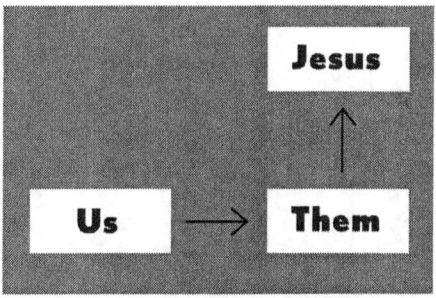

Now both of these perspectives are correct. The trouble is that evangelicals have tended to develop our theology for missions based on Matthew 28 – to the exclusion of Matthew 25. Which means *it is easy to for us see ourselves as people of God, but it is much more difficult for us to see others – especially strangers with strange beliefs and behaviours – as people of God.*

Jesus was aware of this problem and went out of his way to help people see others – especially strangers with strange beliefs and behaviours – as people of God. Let me tell you a story.

> On one occasion an expert in the law stood up to test Jesus. "Teacher," he asked, "what must I do to inherit eternal life?"
>
> "What is written in the Law?" he replied. "How do you read it?"
>
> He answered: "'Love the Lord your God with all your

heart and with all your soul and with all your strength and with all your mind'; and, 'Love your neighbor as yourself.'"

"You have answered correctly," Jesus replied. "Do this and you will live."

But he wanted to justify himself, so he asked Jesus, "And who is my neighbor?"

In reply Jesus said: "A man was going down from Jerusalem to Jericho, when he fell into the hands of robbers. They stripped him of his clothes, beat him and went away, leaving him half dead. A priest happened to be going down the same road, and when he saw the man, he passed by on the other side. So too, a Levite, when he came to the place and saw him, passed by on the other side. But a Samaritan, as he traveled, came where the man was; and when he saw him, he took pity on him. He went to him and bandaged his wounds, pouring on oil and wine. Then he put the man on his own donkey, took him to an inn and took care of him. The next day he took out two silver coins and gave them to the innkeeper. 'Look after him,' he said, 'and when I return, I will reimburse you for any extra expense you may have.'

"Which of these three do you think was a neighbor to the man who fell into the hands of robbers?"

The expert in the law replied, "The one who had mercy on him."

Jesus told him, "Go and do likewise." (Luke 10: 25-37).

Question: Now what would you say is the moral of this story?

Answer 1: We need to show mercy to others. (Yes, but there is more.)

Answer 2: We need to show mercy to those who are not the same as us. (Yes, but there is more.)

Answer 3: We need to realise that sometimes the only way we are going to learn about the need to show mercy to those who are not the same as us is if we are taught by a righteous stranger from a religion other than our own.

Jesus says that at the end of the day he will assess us, the generosity of our hearts and the quality of our work, by the way we treat the 'strangers' we meet – people that we think have 'strange' beliefs and 'strange' behaviours. (For Christians this includes all non-Christians!)

Jesus says:

> When the Son of Man comes in his glory, and all the angels with him, he will sit on his throne in heavenly glory. All the nations will be gathered before him, and he will separate the people one from another as a shepherd separates the sheep from the goats. He will put the sheep on his right and the goats on his left.
>
> Then the King will say to those on his right, "Come,

you who are blessed by my Father; take your inheritance, the kingdom prepared for you since the creation of the world. For I was hungry and you gave me something to eat, I was thirsty and you gave me something to drink, I was a stranger and you invited me in, I needed clothes and you clothed me, I was sick and you looked after me, I was in prison and you came to visit me."

Then the righteous will answer him, "Lord, when did we see you hungry and feed you, or thirsty and give you something to drink? When did we see you a stranger and invite you in, or needing clothes and clothe you? When did we see you sick or in prison and go to visit you?"

The King will reply, "I tell you the truth, whatever you did for one of the least of these brothers of mine, you did for me."

Then he will say to those on his left, "Depart from me, you who are cursed, into the eternal fire prepared for the devil and his angels. For I was hungry and you gave me nothing to eat, I was thirsty and you gave me nothing to drink, I was a stranger and you did not invite me in, I needed clothes and you did not clothe me, I was sick and in prison and you did not look after me."

They also will answer, "Lord, when did we see you hungry or thirsty or a stranger or needing clothes or sick or in prison, and did not help you?"

He will reply, "I tell you the truth, whatever you did not do for one of the least of these, you did not do for me."

Then they will go away to eternal punishment, but the righteous to eternal life (Matthew 25:31-46).

Jesus says, "Whatever you do for one of the least of these brothers (and sisters) of mine, you do for me." My friend Nimmi Hutnik (1991) points out there are four distinctly different attitudes people in a majority faith (like Christianity) can take to our brothers and sisters from minority faiths, that can be illustrated as follows.

Attitudes	1. Assimilative	4. Receptive
Majority > Minority Relations	Us – Yes Them – *No*	Us – Yes Them – Yes
	2. Reactive	3. Alienated
Majority > Minority Relations	Us – *No* Them – Yes	Us – *No* Them – *No*

If we are *alienated* we are 'anti-majority and anti-minority' and would probably say, "to hell with everybody!"

If are *assimilative* we are 'pro-majority and anti-minority' and would typically say, "The majority culture is good, but minority cultures are bad, and they should just adopt the majority culture."

If we are *reactive* we are 'pro-minority and anti-majority' and would typically say, "Minority cultures are good, but the majority culture is bad, and should just adapt to minority cultures".

If we are *receptive* we are both 'pro-majority and pro-minority' would tend to say, "Both the majority culture and minority cultures are good, and we need to work out a way forward, brace the best of both worlds."

Miroslav Volf is a Croatian. His family, along with hundreds of thousands of others in the former Yugoslavia – Croatia, Serbia and Bosnia – have been torn apart by civil war, and what has come to be known as *ethnic cleansing*. Volf says that to embrace the way of Christ, is not a way to exclude others as others, for example as non-Christians. Quite the contrary. He says that to *embrace the way of Christ is a way of embracing others – a way of including those that are usually excluded* (in Andrews 1999, pp. 189-192). Volf says:

> A refusal to embrace the other, in her otherness, and a desire to purge her from one's world by ostracism or oppression, deportation or liquidation, is ... an exclusion of God; for our God 'is a God who loves strangers!' Some say "too much blood has been shed for us to live together." But, Christ calls us to embrace the other, because the 'only way to peace is through embrace' (in Andrews 1999, p. 191).

An embrace always involves "a double movement," Volf says, "of *aperture* and *closure*."

I open my arms to create space in myself for the other. The open arms are a sign of discontent at being myself only, and of a desire to include the other. They are an invitation to the other to come in and feel at home with me, to belong to me ... *In an embrace I close my arms around the other – not tightly, so as to crush her, or assimilate her forcefully into myself; but gently, so as to tell her that I do not want to be without her in her otherness* (in Andrews 1999, p. 191).

"An embrace," Volf says,

> is a *sacrament* of a (Christ-like) personality. It mediates the interiority of the other in me, and my complex identity that includes the other, a unity in diversity .... *It is 'a microcosm of the new creation' Christ envisaged* (in Andrews 1999, p. 191).

2. A Christ-like way of embracing a multifaith society

Developing openness to embrace

Here are a few tips on how we can embrace one another in our multi-faith communities, as what Desmond Tutu calls "the Rainbow People of God."

Meditate on the oneness of the human family. There are not many races, there is only *one* race. Beneath the differences we are all the same. The most personal is the most universal. We all want to love and be loved.

Celebrate heterogeneity rather than homogeneity. There is one whole, but there are many parts. The differences may seem quite superficial, but they are actually quite significant. The universal is not uniform, but multiform. We all want to live different ways, not be forced to live the same way as everyone else.

Recognise the contradictions in our values. We need to be aware of any egocentricity that could subvert our work for unity, and any ethnocentricity that could subvert our work for diversity, that may be operating unconsciously in the way that we live our lives.

Acknowledge the limitations in our knowledge. We need to be aware of our ignorance. We all have blindspots which, by definition, we cannot see ourselves. So we need to listen to the feedback that we get from others, in order to see the way we live our lives as others see us.

Revel in the role of a learner at large. To start with, we need to keep our mouths shut and our eyes and ears open. If we must speak, we need to ask open-ended questions, rather than make statements that close down discussion. A closed person cannot learn from anyone, not even a dear friend. But an open person can learn from everyone, even a complete stranger.

Delight in the whole world as a teacher. If we are willing to learn, the whole world will be willing to teach us. It can teach us not only a whole range of ways to talk but, also, with each new way of talking, can teach us a new way of thinking. Each new set of vocabulary gives us a new set of categories to be able to understand our world anew.

Relish developing another worldview. Our worldview isn't the only worldview. In spite of the propaganda of our various religions, none of us has a monopoly on verity. It can be really exciting to compare and contrast the vast array of perspectives that the worldviews of our numerous traditions provide.

Enjoy exploring the same world differently. We need to take every chance we can get to look at the world through another's eyes. In spite of our fears, we need to have the courage to step out into the unknown with others as our guide. Then we will be able to experience a myriad of unexpected wonders inherent in our otherwise predictable world.

Rejoice in the possibility of synthesis. Together we can work towards a community world that is a unique combination of all our cultures, the best of all possible worlds. Not single cropping, but companion planting. Not agri-culture, but perma-culture. Not ethnic cleansing, but inclusive living. Not mono-culture, but multi-culture. Not concrete jungle, but global village. We alone can do it. But we cannot do it alone.

Engage in the practice of satya, ahimsa and tapasya. The first step towards a community world is *satya*. Satya means seeking after the truth in every situation. Without such seeking there can be no comprehension of the potential, let alone the realisation of the potential, that is intrinsic to every situation.

The second step towards a community world is *ahimsa*. Ahimsa means seeking a way forward together, with everyone who can help us, in a way that is not harmful to the welfare of anyone, whether they are part of the group helping us or not.

The third step towards a community world is *tapasya*. Tapasya means seeking a way forward together, and continuing to seek it, until we find it, accepting the pain of the painstaking process, as the price we are gladly willing to pay, in order to find a way to become the "Rainbow People of God."[3]

Developing practices for embrace[4]

Practice 1: 'Treat others as you would be treated yourself.'

People of all religions, all over the world know that there are no short cuts; that there are no quick fixes; and that we cannot hope to develop community unless we *do unto others as we would have them do unto us.*

The Golden Rule	Hinduism "Never do to others what would pain you." Panchatantra 3.104	Buddhism "Hurt not others with that which hurts yourself." Udana 5.18	Zoroastrianism "Do not to others what is not well for oneself." Shayast-na-shayast 13.29
Jainism "One who neglects existence disregards their own existence." Mahavira	Confucianism "Do not impose on others what you do not yourself desire." Analects 12.2	Taoism "Regard your neighbour's loss or gain as your own loss or gain." Tai Shang Kan Ying Pien	Baha'i "Desire not for any-one the things you would not desire for yourself." Baha'Ullah 66
Judaism "What is hateful to you do not do to your neighbour." Talmud, Shabbat, 31a	Christianity "Do unto others as you would have them do unto you." Matthew 7:12	Islam "Do unto all people as you would they should do to you." Mishkat-el-Masabih	Sikhism "Treat others as you would be treated yourself." Adi Granth

McKenna (2000)

---

[3] These terms are in Hindi. I learned to take these steps in a multi-faith community in India.

[4] Adapted from Andrews 1990, pp. 12-13.

In Jainism the call is *descriptive*. "One who neglects existence disregards their own existence." In Taoism the call is *instructive*. "Regard your neighbour's loss or gain as our own loss or gain." In Hinduism, Buddhism, Zoroastrianism, Confucianism, Judaism and Baha'i the call is *imperative* and it is framed *in negative terms*. "Never do to others what would pain you." "Hurt not others with that which hurts yourself." "What is hateful to you do not do to your neighbour." "Do not impose on others what you do not yourself desire." "Desire not for anyone the things you would not desire for yourself." While in Christianity, Islam and Sikhism the call is *imperative* and it is framed in *positive terms*. "Do unto others as you would have them do unto you." "Do unto all people as you would they should do to you." "Treat others as you would be treated yourself."[5]

Consider your answer to these questions.

- What version of the saying can you relate to best?
- How do you interpret this saying?
- Why is it important to you?

Practice 2: 'Not as you are treated – but as you would be treated.'

Now, to *treat others as we would like to be treated* is, as we all know, not at all easy. But to *treat others as we would like to be treated* when others have *not treated us as we would like to be treated* is excruciatingly difficult to do. Yet *treating others as we would like to be treated* is at the very heart of compassionate

---

[5]Adapted from Andrews 1990, pp. 12-13.

community work!

Some modern psychologists like Sigmund Freud would say "to treat others as we would like them to treat us" when others have "not treated us as we would like to be treated" is *impossible*. But other modern psychiatrists, like Viktor Frankl, would say it *is not only possible, but it is most imperative where it would seem most impossible!*

> We who lived in the concentration camps can remember those who walked through the huts comforting others, giving away their last piece of bread. They may have been few in number but *they offer sufficient proof that everything can be taken from us but the last of human freedoms – the freedom to choose our spirit in any circumstance* (in Kornfield 2002, p. 7).

While Sigmund Freud tells us to "love thy neighbour as thy neighbour loves thee," rather than "love thy neighbour as thyself," Mahatma Gandhi insists that taking 'an eye for an eye' will only end up creating a short-sighted society in which the blind lead the blind.

The Buddha, Siddartha Gautama, gently reminds us, "Hatred never ceases by hatred, but by love alone is healed. This is the ancient and eternal law of the universe" (in Kornfield 2002, p. 5). And Martin Luther King, the great 20th century civil rights campaigner, warns us "never to succumb to the temptation of becoming bitter. *As you press for justice, be sure to move with dignity and discipline, using only the instrument of love*" (in Kornfield 2002, p. 82).

So the art at the heart of community work is learning to overcome hatred with love.

Consider your answer to the following questions:

- What do you think about the idea of *overcoming hatred with love*?
- How do you feel about using only the *instrument of love* yourself?

Developing disciplines for embrace[6]

Overcoming hatred using the instrument of love in the struggle for justice requires learning the disciplines of the heart:

The disciplines of the heart	
(i)	Grieving
(ii)	Giving Up
(iii)	Forgiving
(iv)	Letting Go
(v)	And Loving

(i) The discipline of grieving

If we are to learn to love in the midst of hate – or any other form of perfidy or duplicity – we need to grieve the tragedy of loving without being loved as we would like, in return.

Grieving is the natural human response to loss. It helps feel the

---
[6] This section is based on Kornfield 2002.

pain of the loss. And, in feeling the pain, helps us acknowledge, integrate, and accept the reality of our loss.

If we do not grieve well, we may get stuck in denying the reality, trying to negotiate our way through a situation that was already decided long ago, or raging against our fate. If we get stuck in denying the situation we are in, trying to negotiate our way out, or raging ferociously against our fate, we simply will not be able to deal with the reality well.

There are many ways to grieve. Some of us prefer to sit with it in silence. Some of us prefer to talk it out. Some of us prefer to sing it through. And others of us prefer just to wail away. Whichever way we prefer to do it, our grief is usually drenched with tears!

A meditation on grieving

Create a comfortable atmosphere, if possible in semi-darkness. Sit on your own, or with a friend. Once seated, attend to your breathing. Take one hand and hold it gently to your heart, as if you are holding a precious but fragile human being in your hands. You are your self. As you continue breathing, bring to mind a loss you grieve. Let the story of the loss unfold. Allow the feelings associated with it to surface and flow. Let the feelings come one by one. Hold them. Name them. And honour them. Touch them tenderly. Treat them kindly. Then let their tears begin to take them away.

> When after heavy rain the storm clouds disperse
> is it not that they've wept themselves clear to the end?

Ghalib[7]

---

[7] in Kornfield 2002, p. 58.

(ii) The discipline of giving up

The idea of giving up is generally repugnant to people working for social change. But in order to work for change well we need to give up many things along the way. Among the many things we need to give up along the way is all hope of a better past.

Maybe things could have been better, maybe they should have been better, but though we might be able to change the future for the better, we simply cannot change the past.

We must not forget the past. We must remember it in order to learn from it. But we cannot live in the past anymore than we can live in the future. We can only live in the present.

It is only as we give up all hope of creating a better past and live our lives as faithfully as we can in the present, that we give ourselves a chance of creating a better future.

A meditation on giving up

Create a comfortable atmosphere, if possible in low light. Sit on your own, or with a friend. Once seated, attend to your breathing. Remember a moment of disappointment in the past. Take a piece of paper and write down the event that occurred. Reflect on the event – what happened and its impact. Then, on a separate piece of paper, write down the main lesson you learned from the event. Put the two pieces of paper side by side – the event and the lesson. Choose to give up trying to change the event, but take the lesson to heart. Put the piece of paper on which you wrote about the event to one side, but hold onto the paper on which you wrote the lesson you learned.

> *It is only as we give up all hope of creating a better past,*
> *and live our lives as faithfully as we can in the present,*
> *that we give ourselves a chance of creating a better future.*

(iii) The discipline of forgiving

We know that we cannot change the past. We know that we cannot undo the pain. However, some of us try to heal the pain we have suffered by inflicting pain on the people who made us suffer. As if their suffering more would somehow result in our suffering less.

But the desire for revenge usually only serves to increase the suffering of the victim. If we do not forgive our tormentors, we will continue to be tortured by our resentment.

Forgiving is not forgetting. We must remember suffering and learn from our suffering. We should not associate with our tormentor, unless we are sure they will not torment us.

Forgiving is not fooling. To the contrary, it's smart. It is a way of maintaining our sanity. As we forgive the unforgivable we release the love that alone can heal the wounds.

A meditation on forgiving

Create a comfortable atmosphere. Set the scene with a small candle. Sit on your own, or with a friend. Once seated, attend to your breathing. Start by visualising the ways you have hurt others. See the pain you have caused others – knowingly or unknowingly. Feel the sorrow, shame, guilt and regret you feel about this. Picture each person that comes to mind, one by one, sense their suffering, and say:

> *I remember many ways I have hurt others.*
> *I recognise the pain I have caused.*
> *I ask for your forgiveness, I ask for your forgiveness,*
> *I ask for your forgiveness.*

Continue by visualising the ways others have hurt you. See the pain others have caused you – knowingly or unknowingly. Feel the sorrow, anger and resentment you feel about this. Picture each person who comes to mind and, as your heart is ready, say to them:

> *I remember many ways others have hurt me.*
> *I have carried this pain in my heart long enough.*
> *To the extent that I am ready, I offer those who hurt me forgiveness.*
> *I offer you my forgiveness, I offer you my forgiveness,*
> *I offer you my forgiveness.*

Forgiving is not a weak reaction, but it is a strong, courageous, constructive response. As it says in the Gita, "If you want to see the brave, look for those who can forgive" (in Kornfield 2002, p. 26).

(iv) The discipline of letting go

Letting go is just letting things be as they are. Not holding onto anything that would hold us back from moving on and becoming the human/humane person we are called to be. When we learn just to let things be as they are they gradually lose their power over us.

Letting go is not cutting off. It is not cutting ourselves off from ourselves, from our memories or our responsibilities. It is not cutting ourselves off from others, from our families or our communities. But it is letting go of our disappointment and despair.

A meditation on letting go

Create a comfortable atmosphere. Set the scene with a small candle and a metal bowl. Sit on your own or with a friend. Once seated, attend to your breathing. Remember some reactions that you feel it is time to let go of. Name them (sadness, resentment, anxiety, anger, etc.). Hold these feelings with tenderness in your heart one more time. Then, when you are ready to let these feelings go, write them down. When the list of feelings you want to let go of is finished, think about the benefits that will come from letting these feelings go – once and for all. Take the paper on which you have written the list of feelings you want to let go of, set them on fire with the candle and burn them in the metal bowl. At the same time, take the paper that you put to one side, on which you had written about the event you wanted to give up, and burn it to ashes in the bowl. As the smoke rises like incense say *Let it go. Let it go. Let it go.*

> *If you let go a little, you will have a little happiness.*
> *If you will let go a lot, you will have a lot of happiness.*

Ajahn Chah [8]

(v) The discipline of loving

Loving is treating others – not as we have been treated – as

---

[8] in Kornfield 2002, p.54.

we would like to be treated. It is extending the same kind of acceptance and respect and resolute positive regard to others that we would like ourselves. It is creating the same kind of opportunities for others to participate in community – and realise their potential – as we would like ourselves.

A meditation on loving

Create a comfortable atmosphere. Set the scene with a small candle. Sit on your own, or with a friend. Once seated, attend to your breathing. Begin with yourself. Picture yourself and pray for yourself repeatedly:

> *May I be filled with loving kindness for myself.*

When you are ready, move on to people you like. Picture them and pray for them repeatedly:

> *May I be filled with loving kindness for you.*

If there are any particular feelings of gratitude you feel for them, just give thanks. When you are ready, move on to people who you don't like. Picture them and pray for them repeatedly:

> *May I be filled with loving kindness for you.*

If there are any particular feelings of irritation you feel for them, hold them gently.

> *Like a caring mother holding the life of her only child so with a heart of loving kindness hold all beings as your beloved children.*

Buddha [9]

---
[9] in Kornfield 2002, p. 70.

3. A Christ-like way to share our faith with people of other Faiths

Before we proceed let me start by emphasising my assumptions.

- God is already there, wherever we may go.
- Jesus is already with people, 'Christians' and 'non-Christians' alike.
- The Spirit is already at work in every situation, whether people know it or not.
- Our role is not to try to convert people, but to simply witness to what we know.

Let me explain what I mean.

God is already there, wherever we may go. We find this in Psalms.

> Where can I go from your Spirit?
> Where can I flee from your presence?
> If I go up to the heavens, you are there;
> if I make my bed in hell, you are there.
> If I rise on the wings of the dawn,
> if I settle on the far side of the sea,
> even there your hand will guide me,
> your right hand will hold me fast
> (Psalm139:7-10)

And we find this in Acts.

> Paul stood up in the meeting of the Areopagus and said:

> "Men of Athens! I see that in every way you are very religious. For as I walked around and looked carefully at your objects of worship, I even found an altar with this inscription: TO AN UNKNOWN GOD. Now what you worship as something unknown I am going to proclaim to you.
>
> "The God who made the world and everything in it is the Lord of heaven and earth and does not live in temples built by hands. And he is not served by human hands, as if he needed anything, because he himself gives all men life and breath and everything else. From one man he made every nation of men, that they should inhabit the whole earth; and he determined the times set for them and the exact places where they should live. God did this so that men would seek him and perhaps reach out for him and find him, though he is not far from each one of us. 'For in him we live and move and have our being.' As some of your own poets have said, 'We are his offspring'" (Acts 17:22-28).

Jesus is already with people, Christians and non-Christians alike, as we find in Colossians.

> For by [Christ] all things were created: things in heaven and on earth, visible and invisible, whether thrones or powers or rulers or authorities; all things were created by him and for him, and in him all things hold together (Colossians 1:16-17).

And we find this in John.

> Through him all things were made; without him nothing was made that has been made. In him was life, and that life was the light of humankind. The light shines in the darkness, and the darkness has not put it out it ... the true light that gives light to every person coming into the world (John 1:3-5,9).

The Spirit is at work in every situation, whether people know it or not, as we find in Romans.

> We know that in all things God works for the good of those who love him, who have been called according to his purpose (Romans 8:28).

And we find this in John, when Jesus said:

> when the Spirit of truth comes, he (sic) will guide you into all truth. He (sic) will bring glory to me by taking from what is mine and making it known to you (John 16:13-14).

Our role is not to try to convert people, but to witness to what we know. Our responsibility as a Christian is NOT to try to convert anyone BUT to simply *witness to Christ*.

Our role is to witness. Jesus said, "you will receive power when the Holy Spirit comes on you; and you will be my witnesses in Jerusalem, and in all Judea and Samaria, and to the ends of the earth" (Acts 1:8). Some of us have taken Christ's call to *witness* – to *evangelisation* – as a call to *proselytisation*.

The goal of *proselytisation* is for us to convince as many people as possible to join our cause. In seeking to accomplish our goal, we tend to treat people as faceless targets – 'potential trophies' for us to 'win'. We do not treat people as people. If we meet their needs, it is not so much to 'help them win', but to 'help us win them over'.

Christ advocated *evangelisation* – sharing the good news of God's radical commitment to a sacrificial concern for the welfare of the other – but Christ totally repudiated *proselytisation* – precisely because it did not demonstrate God's radical commitment to the sacrificial concern for the welfare of the other (Matthew 23:15).

If we are to witness to God's radical commitment to a sacrificial concern for the welfare of the other, like Christ did, then – like Christ – we will need to totally repudiate all proselytisation.

The best way to witness is not by what you say, but what you do. "Let your light shine before others, that they may see your good deeds and praise your Father in heaven" (Matthew 5:16). If you want to talk about your faith, there are five ways you can share your faith sensitively with others. Try starting with the more simple and moving on to the more complicated.

(i) Tell your own story

If people ask you to, you can tell them about your own journey.

- Make it personal. The most personal is the most universal.
- Be sincere. Make sure it's a drama not an advertisement.
- Say it as it is. No hype. No pretense. No clichés.

- If they are happy to, ask them to tell you their journey too.

This is my story.

*As a toddler I related to Jesus as a **relative**.*

My parents were pious people. My father was a pastor, and my mother was 'in the ministry' too. We were a close family, and my parents talked to us about Jesus as if he were a member of the family.

I don't recall seeing Jesus at our home. But Dad and Mum told us all about him. Each night before we went to sleep they'd read us a story about him, and show us pictures of him from an old storybook.

I can still remember those pictures of Jesus even now. There was one of him carrying a lamb he'd found on his shoulders. And another of him sitting with some kids – which was my favourite – because the kid on his knee looked a lot like me!

*As a child I related to Jesus as a **friend**.*

My parents migrated from England to Australia when I was eight years old. I was uprooted from the only place that I knew. And separated from all the relatives I loved. With the exception of Jesus.

Coming over on the boat, someone played 'Somewhere Over The Rainbow' when we crossed the equator. But the antipodes proved to be anything but the magical Land of Oz for me.

It was uncool to wear shoes to school. And trying to run around the playground in the midday sun – on blistering-hot rock-hard bitumen – on my little, pink, soft, bare feet – was torture.

What made matters worse, was that at that time in Australia, it was a crime to have a posh English accent – and I was beaten unmercifully for being a 'smartmouthed pommie bastard.'

Often I felt that Jesus was the only friend I had in the world.

*As an adolescent I related to Jesus as a **hero**.*

When I read the gospels, I saw Jesus in a whole new light. He struck me as a man's man. He said what he meant and meant what he said. He believed in love and justice and stood up bravely for his beliefs.

So Jesus became my role model. And I took every chance I could to 'be like Jesus' and 'do a Jesus.'

There was a little kid in our neighbourhood that everybody thought was a few sandwiches short of a picnic. All the kids used to pick on him; but there was one big kid in particular that used to pick on him a lot.

"What would Jesus do?" I asked myself. "He'd lay his body on the line to stop the poor blighter from being bullied," I told myself. So I vowed, that next time I saw him being attacked, I'd intervene.

As it turned out, when I did step in, I got beaten to a pulp and had to be rushed off to hospital. But my bruises only served to strengthen my admiration for the man who laid down his life for his friends.

*As an adult I related to Jesus as a **guru**.*

I went to university in the 60s, when revolution was all the rage. And agreed with much of Marx's analysis of society. But thought the solutions to problems Christ proposed were far more radical than Marx.

In the 70s I went to India, along with the rest of my generation. I studied Krishna, Moses, Buddha, and Mohammed. Much of what they said was the truth. But to me, Christ was the truth of which they spoke.

So I have spent most of my life setting up intentional, multi-cultural, inter-religious communities based on the uniquely radical, outrageously inclusive, nonviolent principles of the Rabbi from Nazareth.

And at present, my family and I are part of an inner city network called the Waiters Union, which is committed to developing a discipleship community with disadvantaged groups of people in our home town.

(ii) Host a round table discussion

Here are some steps I recommend to start a round table discussion.

- Find out if anyone is interested in having a faith-based conversation.

- Settle on a topic of conversation e.g. God. Faith. Prayer. Compassion.
- Invite no more than 10 people for a round table discussion.
- Make sure they all know it is a discussion not a debate.
- Create a friendly circle around a table for the discussion.
- Encourage everyone to speak and everyone to listen.
- Go around the table, giving each person five minutes to talk about the topic.
- After everyone has had their say, sit quietly with what they have said.
- Reflect for a few moments, then have a cup of tea or coffee.
- Encourage people over the cuppa to share what they have learnt.
- Before people leave, plan the next meeting.

These are my experiences of round table discussions.

I used to live in a multi-cultural inter-faith community in Delhi dedicated to following the way of Jesus. Not surprisingly the majority of us were Christians. But our household also included Hindus, Muslims, Buddhists and Jains.

As you'd expect, every meal that we ate together became a round table discussion on politics and religion. The only problem we ever had was one we always have at round tables on politics and religion: making sure the Christians didn't dominate the discussion.

When we came back to Brisbane we began to host special round table discussions. We'd invite people we knew from different religious traditions to come to our house once a fortnight for what we called our *multi-cultural inter-faith dialogue meeting*.

One evening I will never forget. The group – most of whom were born overseas, and the majority of whom had been forced to flee to Australia as refugees – decided to talk about *how our religion helped us maintain our humanity in dehumanising circumstances*.

It was a very painful, but very beautiful time, as Hindus, Muslims, Jews, and Christians all shared their stories of how God had kept them sane through the insanity of torture and trauma. Ange and I felt there was so much we could learn from our faith-full refugee friends.

One of our friends, Vinod, a high caste Hindu, came to a point where he put his trust in Jesus through round table discussions and went on to work with World Vision in Thailand.

(iii) Pray empathically with and for people

Most people don't like you preaching at them. But most people don't mind you praying with them. Here is a suggested process for praying empathically.

- If someone presents with a problem, ask if you can pray with them. If they say no, respect their wishes, and let it go. If they say yes, pray as empathically as you can.
- Ask the Spirit to put you in touch with their pain.

- Remember what they said (their issues). Remember how they said it (their emotions). Remember the language that they used to describe their feelings.

- Then say a prayer to God on their behalf, empathically expressing their feelings in their language so that at the end they can say that's what they wanted to say!

This is my experience of praying empathetically.

Some time back a lady talked to me about the hopelessness that many people she knew felt as they struggled for authentic transformation. I wondered if Madie was reflecting her own sense of hopelessness, but did not raise the issue.

A few days later Madie called on the phone. She was desperate. I dropped everything, went and picked her up and brought her home. When Madie arrived at our place, she found that she couldn't contain the pain anymore, and her sense of hopelessness simply exploded all over the kitchen. She wept like a soul tortured in hell, who could endure her hell no longer.

Ange and I embraced Madie as she wept over the years of accumulated brutality that she had suffered at the hands of an abusive husband. We wept together, then prayed, voicing her pain to God. There, at the kitchen table, Madie began to breathe out the hurt and breathe in the healing.

That night we didn't get much sleep. Every time Madie drifted off to sleep she would relive the torment in her dreams and wake up screaming. She would leap out of bed and pace the floor seeking peace. By morning we were all exhausted.

For years Madie had borne this pain alone believing that no one would understand. Even if they could understand, they could never share the pain. And even if they could share the pain, how could they ever help her rise from the depths of despair?

But now she had spoken of her pain. We had provided the time and space for the pain deep inside her to surface in our presence. We had tried to understand and share her pain, even if that understanding and sharing was incomplete.

Through prayer, Madie began to be able to face her pain, without so much despair, believing that, perhaps, there might be a life beyond the death of all her hopes after all.

And, in the courage and strength that hope always imparts, Madie began the difficult task of putting the pieces of her shattered life back together again, bit by bit.

It is more than ten years since Ange and I prayed with Madie at our table in the kitchen at our house in Highgate Hill. And in those ten years Madie has continued to deal with her trauma, and the issues of that it raised for her, in the light of the hope that she experiences in prayer. She often says, "Prayer doesn't make it painless, but it does make it possible for us to deal with our pain."

In working through her own issues Madie has been able to find a way of helping other people work with their issues. So Madie is now a fully qualified social worker who specialises in difficult cases, helping people cope with everything from frightful cruelty through to horrifying cancer (Andrews 2001 pp. 126-129).

(iv) Develop meaningful mutual relationships

Most people share most meaningfully in the context of mutual relationships. I don't think we should just develop relationships in order to share our faith. By definition those relationships would be instrumental, not genuinely mutual. But I think that we should develop lots of genuinely mutual relationships. And if our faith is meaningful to us – and to our friends – it is inevitable that sooner or later in the context of our mutuality we will have a chat about faith.

When we do have a chat about our faith I have the following suggestions.

- Talk about Christ in a way that is always authentically Christ-like.
- Never let our passion for our faith render us insensitive to our friends' thoughts and feelings.
- If we have any doubts about whether what we want to say is Christ-like, we shouldn't say it. We can't unsay what we say, but we can say more later if we want to.

This is my experience of developing a mutually meaningful relationship.

I remember the day I met Prem at the university. An Indian who had recently arrived in Australia, Prem was a migrant, a long way from his country, his culture, and his religion.

When I met him I went up to him and said, "Sat sri akal ji" – which means "God is truth" – a Sikh greeting in the Punjabi language. He was thrilled I was familiar with his religion.

I told Prem I was very glad to meet a fellow believer, as many of the people in the department were unbelievers. Prem appreciated I was respectful of his faith in God.

I suggested that one way we could encourage each other might be to get together for prayer once a week. We agreed to meet by the river every Wednesday before work.

The first week we met, I invited Prem to lead in prayer. And he prayed a beautiful prayer from his Scriptures, the Guru Granth Sahib. I nodded in agreement with everything I could agree with in the prayer, and let anything I disagreed with go through to the keeper.

Prem then invited me to lead in prayer. And I did so. Praying for him and his family. When I finished, Prem said "Aree, Bhai, you talk to God like he is your friend." And I replied saying "My guru, Jesus, taught us to pray to God as a friend."

Prem promptly said he was interested to know more about Jesus. I suggested that if he wanted to learn more about Jesus that he read the Gospels and I lent him my Bible.

The second week Prem came back saying he had been reading the Gospels and loved the way Jesus got stuck into corrupt priests, adding, "The priests in my religion are so corrupt."

At that point many Christians make the mistake of playing *my religion is better than yours.* But we need to remember that *anything bad in other religions you can find in Christianity and anything good in Christianity you can find in other religions.* We are not called to witness to Christianity as a religion. We are called to witness to Jesus – who is over and above and sometimes over and against all religions – including Christianity.

So I didn't say, "Yes, the priests in your religion are corrupt, but the priests in mine are not." Instead I said, "Many of the priests in all religions, including my own, are corrupt. But one of the things that is unique about Jesus is that he was incorruptible."

"Yes," Prem said, "I see. I must read more about him."

The third week Prem came back saying he was loving reading the Gospels and wondered whether he should stop reading his own Scriptures, the Guru Granth Sahib.

At that point it is very important not take unfair advantage of someone's vulnerability and drive a wedge between them and their tradition. We can trust the Spirit to lead people into the truth and to help them reflect critically on their tradition in the same way we do ours.

So I didn't say, "Yes, you should stop reading your Scriptures." Instead I said, "Why don't you continue to read the Gospels and the Guru Granth Sahib side by side, but start to use the Gospels as a framework for critically reflecting on your own tradition. For I believe Jesus will help you affirm all that's good in your religion and confront all that's bad in your religion. Like he does for me."

"Yes," Prem said, 'I'll make sure that I do that."

The fourth week Prem came back saying that Jesus was helping him see his religion in a whole new light. He said that he was using the Gospels as a framework for reflecting on his own tradition, and he was discovering a whole lot of stories within his own tradition that were the same kind of stories that Jesus told. I asked him to tell me one. And this is what he said:

Once there was a sadhu – a saint – who had the reputation of being a truly compassionate soul. Well, one day the sadhu was sitting by his fireside, eating his lunch when a pariah dog came up close to him, and began sniffing round, scrounging for scraps from his lunch. But the sadhu was so engrossed in eating his enjoyable lunch of flat bread chappatti and clarified butter ghee that he didn't notice the dog at all.

Then, all of a sudden, before he knew it, the hungry dog leapt over the fire, lunged at his lunch, tore a fresh, hot, chappatti out of his hands, and ran to the nullah for cover.

The sadhu, realising what had happened, took off after the dog that had stolen his lunch, and ran into the dirty drain where the dog had fled for cover.

When they saw this, the villagers scoffed at the sadhu, saying, "We heard he was a compassionate soul; but see – the sadhu is running like a dog into the nullah to get his chappatti back!"

They were still mocking him when the sadhu returned, all covered in mud from chasing the dog in the dirty drain.

"How did you go?" the villagers asked sarcastically "Well," the Sadhu replied, "it was a hard chase. But I finally caught the dog

who had taken my chappatti – and gave him my ghee."

When they heard what the sadhu said the villagers were stunned into silence.

So the sadhu continued. "Chappattis are so much better with ghee," he said. "But that rascal ran off so quickly he forgot to take the ghee. Thank God I was able to catch the hungry little fellow and give him the ghee to go with the chappatti."

When Prem told me this story I punched the air and cried, "That's it Prem, that's it! That's exactly kind of story Jesus would tell. It's a classic Gospel story full of amazing grace."

This process went on week after week. Then one day Prem came to me and said "Dave, Jesus appeared to me in a dream last night and said 'I am the Way. Follow me.'"

So I said to Prem, "What do you want to do?"

He said, "Well the first step will be for me to go to my Gurudwara (his local Sikh temple) and tell people about my experience and teach them the Lord's Prayer."

So he did (Andrews 2001, pp. 104-107).

(v) Practise a centred set problem solving process

Most relationships with people involve problems and problem solving.

I try to approach problem solving from a Christ-centred perspective.

With Christians, who are not alienated by this, I make this explicit. With non-Christians, who may be alienated, I keep my approach implicit.

I negotiate solving problems on the basis of common sense and consensus.

Because God *is the source of truth, and that truth is written on the hearts of all people* (Romans 2:14-15) and living in the hearts of all people (John 1:9), that *truth is often expressed in the common sense* we speak to each other.

Whenever somebody says something which I believe is Christ-like and true to the heart of God, I *agree* with it. If I do not believe it is Christ-like or in tune with God's heart, I *disagree* with it. Just because I disagree doesn't mean I voice my disagreement. Conflicts, like kisses, should be saved for special occasions.

Every time I agree, I gain a credit in credibility. Every time, I disagree I lose a credit. I want to gain credibility to discuss crucial issues, not lose credibility over incidental issues. I save my credits for the time I need to spend them on a disagreement that is substantive.

Actually, I don't find myself in disagreement as much as others might imagine. I can usually agree with the way sensible people decide to solve their problems.

The times I do find myself in disagreement, I feel perfectly free to express my thoughts because we have agreed to resolve our problems by *consensus,* which means no one coerces anyone else into a course of action they disagree with.

I find that many groups I work with, even those who only use God's name blasphemously, often act in sympathy with his heart. That may seem strange to some. But it may not seem so strange if we remember that all of us, even those of us who don't believe in God, are made in the image of God, an image which though distorted, has not been totally destroyed by our proclivity to stupidity.

So together we can agree to solve problems in a Christ-like way – according to God's agenda – though I may be the only one who recognises it as such.

Once we have resolved a problem and we are rejoicing together, I make explicit the implicit connection between the decision we have made and the prophetic tradition personified in Christ. I love to tell people, particularly those hostile to Christianity, who are celebrating the successful resolution of a problem, that the success was dependent on our having taken the kind of action Jesus Christ advocated. Regardless of their attitudes to Christ, they cannot deny the successful resolution of the problem or disregard the value of the kind of action advocated by Christ – especially when they have just tried it and seen how well works!

I go through this process over and over again. Each time the group makes significant progress towards personal growth and social change, and each time I explain the significance of God's agenda personified in Christ to the process we have just experienced.

As a result, God's agenda increasingly becomes a more credible *point of view.*

Sooner or later, usually later, God's agenda, personified in Christ, becomes such a credible point of view that it moves from being *one point of view among many* that are credible to *the one point of view by which all others are judged*. The indicator that this time has arrived is when people ask about God's agenda *before* they make a decision rather than *after*.

At this stage it is crucial to know enough about the prophetic tradition in general, and the gospels in particular, to be able to find a parable, a story or a principle that relates directly to the problem the group is seeking to resolve.

If people adopt the agenda of God, personified in Christ, as the agenda for their decision-making, they have made a significant transition. The agenda of God has moved from being a *point of view* to the *point of reference*. The process of conversion to Christ as a person – but not necessarily Christianity as a religion – has begun. And, as part and parcel of this conversion process, is the incredible potential for authentic, sustainable, community transformation.

Let me tell you a story of how such a process took place among a group of people who were not only non-Christians, but decidedly anti-Christian.

Together with my friends, we decided to get involved with a bunch of squatters. They were totally demoralised. They had no jobs. With no jobs they could not afford to pay rent. Because they had nowhere to live they squatted on land beside the road. Because this was illegal, they were constantly harassed by the police who would either demand a bribe, or break down their hutments and beat them up. As a result they were constantly on the move, trying desperately to stay one step ahead of the police. But there weren't many places they could go, so they always wound up back where they started, ready to go through the cycle again.

We got to know this group. Bonds of friendship formed between individuals and their families. They were demoralised, but what they lacked in dignity, they more than made up for in guts. Their struggle against seemingly overwhelming odds was fought with lots of courage and lots of laughter. We were encouraged and strengthened by their infectious style of heroism and sense of humour. They may have been demoralised, but they taught us valuable lessons about the morality of survival. As our friendships deepened, we not only learned from them the art of survival in an urban slum, we began to feel the anguish they felt in their struggle to survive. As we discussed with them the issues they had to face every day of their lives, we decided to work together with them and see if together we could find some long term solutions that would not only minimise the anguish associated with their struggle for survival, but also increase their chances of surviving.

One day the group decided something had to be done about the continuing police harassment. Some wanted to attack the police station immediately with bricks. Bricks were a common means of settling disputes in the slum. As a conflict resolution technique, the people considered it a knockout. We encouraged the people to envisage in their minds what the result of throwing bricks through the window of the police station might be. They concluded that it would probably result in an even more violent visit by the police. The people began to have very serious doubts about the effectiveness of bricks as a conflict resolution technique.

So we began to discuss other possibilities for solving the problem. Someone suggested inviting the police over for a cup of tea and discussing the matter. The squatters treated the idea with scorn, but we supported it. The longer we discussed it, the more support it got. Eventually the police were invited. To start with, you could cut the air with a knife, but the tension was soon dispelled with a couple of jokes. The squatters and the police ended up having an amicable chat and as a result decided to call a truce. The squatters agreed not to cause the police any trouble and the police agreed not to beat up the squatters.

After the police had gone, we had a talk about, how the problem had been resolved. During the discussion one of us mentioned that the problem had been resolved exactly how Christ had suggested such problems be resolved. He said, "Bless those who curse you" and, "If your enemy is thirsty give him a drink," which is exactly what the group had done by inviting the police for a cup of tea. Everyone treated it as a joke. They were embarrassed that they had done anything remotely religious, even if unintentionally. But the squatters remembered the way they had solved the problem with the police and they also remembered that it was the way Christ suggested problems be solved.

Time went by. Week after week, month after month, we worked on a whole range of problems together. Everything from getting a regular water supply to improving nutrition and sanitation. Each time we resolved a problem together it would be on the basis of common sense and consensus. After the effecttive resolution of each of these problems, we would discuss how the decision we had taken fitted with the way Christ advocated that problems be dealt with. After each successful resolution of a problem there would be a celebration. It was during this euphoria that we would always explain how the success was contingent upon our having worked in harmony with God's agenda, as personified in Christ, and always there would be the mock groans, that if we carried on the way we were going, that they would all be Christians before too long!

About a year after inviting the police for a cup of tea, the council decided to clean up the city. Cleaning up the city meant getting rid of the squatters. They were notified to leave immediately. But they had nowhere to go. Then they got news that really freaked them out. The bulldozers were on the way. In a panic they considered their options. But there didn't seem to be any. Any promising options had to be discarded because they felt too powerless to make them happen. "It's typical," they concluded. "Those big people can push us little people around as much as they like and there is not a thing we can do about it." We were tempted to agree. Things looked hopeless. But somehow we knew that we had to believe that the impossible was possible. "Surely there is something we can do!" one person said hopefully. "Yeah?" asked one of the squatters. "What? What would Christ do about it?"

Raising Christ, as a possible point of reference for solving the problem, had never happened before in our discussions with the squatters. It was a crucial time for this group. A time when Christ might become more than just one point of view among many points of view; a time when Christ might become the point of reference for all their problem solving. The time when the group might be converted to a faith in Christ through which their life might be transformed. It all hinged upon finding a Christ story that the group could use to help them to do something about their situation.

I racked my brain, wondering where on earth you could find a story in the gospels that helped a group of squatters deal with the threat of eviction backed by the might of bulldozers. I don't remember who it was, but someone suggested a story they thought may help. It was the story Christ told of a little old widow who was finding it difficult to get justice from a big crooked judge. She finally got justice by knocking on his door at all hours of the night for week after week. As we discussed the story with them, hope began to rise out of their hopelessness. As hope was born, so was a new sense of power.

They started discussing the possible solutions in a whole new light. They decided to take up a petition to present to the city council and to persist until they got a fair hearing. They gathered hundreds of signatures and organised a march to the city council administration centre to present the petitions. Then they followed up on the people who could change the decision.

Finally, through perseverance they had learned about in the story of the little old widow and the big crooked judge, they were granted an alternative place to stay where the community would have their own houses on their own land. Not only that, the council would help pay the expenses of their move.

It was more than they had ever dreamed possible. The move also opened up a whole host of new doors. Not only did they now have their own homes on their own land, they could now develop their own education, health and employment programs. With the decrease in demoralisation came an observable increase in morale – and morality – in the community. There was a marked decrease in domestic violence and child abuse. People engaged in more constructive forms of work and less destructive forms of recreation. There was a marked increase in happier couples and healthier children. Fewer people went to untimely graves. And those who survived not only lived longer, they also lived fuller lives. And at the centre of all this activity was a group in the community who remembered that the personal growth and social change had come about because they had followed the agenda of God, personified in Christ. This group weren't content with their growth so far. They looked into the future and saw some of the changes that were possible, if they were to follow in the footsteps of Christ and, like him, live wholeheartedly for God, and his agenda of love and justice (Andrews 2001, pp. 148-158).

Conclusion

Wherever we go, whoever we meet, whatever we say, it's always important for us to be mindful of Jesus' single essential rule for engagement and dialogue.

> How can you say to your neighbour, 'Let me take the speck out of your eye,' when all the time there is a plank in your own eye? You hypocrite, *first take the plank out of your own eye, and then (secondly) you will see clearly to remove the speck from your neighbour's eye* (Matthew 7:4-5).

References

Andrews, D. (1990). *In-situ community education.*

Andrews, D. (1999). *Christi-Anarchy.* Oxford: Lion Publishing.

Andrews, D. (2001). *Not religion, but love.* Oxford: Lion Publishing.

Brueggemann, W. (1997). *Cadences from home: Preaching among exiles.* Louisville, KY: Westminster/John Knox Press.

Hutnik, N. (1991). *Ethnic minority identity: A social psychological perspective.* Oxford: Oxford University Press.

Kornfield, J. (2002). *The art of forgiveness, lovingkindness and peace.* Sydney: Rider.

McKenna, P. (2000). *The golden rule* (poster). Dayton, OH: Pflaum Publishing Group.

Mathison, S. (2000). Unpublished masters thesis, Bible College of Queensland, Brisbane.

LIBERATION THEOLOGIANS SPEAK TO EVANGELICALS: A THEOLOGY AND PRAXIS OF SERVING THE POOR[1]

Dr Charles Ringma

Introduction

There are a number of inter-related themes that form the heart of this chapter. But the heartbeat has to do with God's love and passion for the poor and our invitation to enter into that passion and to live that out in a costly discipleship marked by grace and joy.

First and foremost, I wish to bring some Latin American Liberation theologians into critical dialogue with a major section of Evangelicalism, namely the Lausanne movement[2] (Stott 1997). The reason for this is that I believe that these theologians can help us, as Evangelicals, to deepen our understanding of and commitment to the poor.

Thus this chapter is a constructive enterprise.

This kind of dialogue will not be easy, however. Many Evangelicals view Liberation theology with grave concern and

---

[1] This essay was originally published in the compendium of the Fourth ATS Theological Forum, L. Wanak (ed.), 2008, The Church and Poverty in Asia, Manila: OMF Lit. pp. 7-53.

[2] The Lausanne Movement is a worldwide movement that mobilises Evangelical leaders to collaborate for world evangelisation. The International Congress on World Evangelization first gathered in Lausanne, Switzerland in 1974 around the theme, "Let The Earth Hear His Voice." Since then the Lausanne Covenant has challenged Christians to work together to make Jesus Christ known throughout the world.

often with deep suspicion. It is, therefore, possible that the voice and witness of the Liberation theologians will be prematurely dismissed,[3] just like a Muslim Indonesian rice farmer will not readily be heard by a Protestant Australian wheat farmer, particularly not when the former raises concerns in relation to the latter.

It must be recognised that my overall purpose is *not* generally to defend Liberation theology as a system or as a whole. I am all too aware of the many critics who have raised all sorts of concerns about this theology (McGovern 1991; Bell 2001). My purpose is more narrow and specific. I wish to suggest that Evangelical theologians, pastors, urban poor workers and community development personnel can learn from the theology and praxis of some of the Liberation theologians[4] regarding a more deeply Biblically informed vision of serving the poor and a more grounded commitment in the work of justice and social transformation on behalf of the poor.

Secondly, in order to ground this dialogue between the Liberation theologians and Evangelicals, I seek to do two things. I believe it is important to restate the Biblical vision regarding God's concern for the poor. This, after all, is fundamentally normative for the Christian community. And in the light of that witness we can see to what extent both groups reflect the power and the challenges that the Biblical witness brings.

At the same time, I believe it is important to listen to the witness

---

[3] The major, but largely unfounded, criticisms of Latin American Liberation theology are: the gospel is de-emphasized; faith is cast in too political terms; Marxist social theories are used; and concepts of violence to bring about social change are present in some of their writings (Ferm 1998, pp. 100-116).

[4] It is not my purpose to draw on global Liberation theologies (Rowland 1999) or on Third world Liberation theologies in general (Ferm 1986). I am only engaging some of the key Latin American Liberation theologians.

of the church's long march in history. Throughout this history Christians have always served the poor (Troeltsch 1960). This long history demonstrates both the faithfulness and creativity of the faith community and the failure of the church in living out the Biblical witness regarding service to the poor. Thus this will further situate both Evangelicals and the Liberation theologians regarding this long witness.

That this history of the church has been an uneven, potted and flawed history will not surprise us. The church has been a passionate institution when it has been revitalised and renewed theologically, spiritually and missionally. It has also been a moribund community when it has become introspective, formalised and lacking in missional purpose.

While all the larger denominational groupings within the Christian church reflect this faithfulness/failure movement, and Evangelicals at times have served the poor well,[5] especially in times of renewal, such as the Wesleyan revival (Oliver 1930; Snyder 1980; Hynson 1984), I believe that overall Evangelicals have not fared well. The reasons for this are fourfold. I don't believe that Evangelicals have developed a robust theology of the poor. Furthermore, their focus has always tended to be more spiritual than also social. The same criticism can be made about Evangelicals in relation to the environment – more spiritual than also concerned for the physical world. Moreover, their response to the poor has often been driven more by pragmatics than by a Biblical-theological vision. Finally, in the Evangelical documents of the Lausanne movement service to the poor is more incidental and often peripheral.

---

[5] For some of the responses in the UK in the 19th and 20th centuries see Coutts 1978; Himmelfarb 1991; Lewis 2001, and in the US see Magnuson 1990.

In contrast, as we shall see in the substance of this chapter, the Liberation theologians have a much richer theology of the poor, reflect the Biblical vision more faithfully and in the church's missional service to the poor reflect a richer tradition than is captured in the Lausanne documents.

This *centrality* regarding the poor in the writings of some of the Liberation theologians is articulated around the following themes.

- Hermeneutically – the Bible is read from the perspective of God's passion for the poor, and as such, it is read not as a book of comfort for the middle classes, but from the underside of history and the vision of God's upside down Kingdom.

- Theologically – theology is structured by seriously engaging God's preferential option for the poor, the Exodus motif and the incarnational mission of Jesus in bringing good news to the poor (Luke 7:22),[6] producing a theology that is fundamentally missional in its basic orientation.

- Spiritually – this hermeneutic and its theology move us from head to heart to embrace a spirituality of descent following that of the great hymn in Philippians 2 which expresses itself in 'evangelical' poverty. This means that Christian theologians, pastors, facilitators, and urban poor workers are willing, for the sake of the

---

[6] In this essay, unless stated otherwise, Scripture taken from New Revised Standard Version Bible, copyright 1989, Division of Christian Education of the National Council of the Churches of Christ in the United States of America. Used by permission. All rights reserved.

gospel, to move to the side of the poor through radical identification. This becomes the central motif for an incarnational spirituality.

- Ecclesiastically – in the Base Ecclesial Communities (BECs) of South America we have seen the formation of the church of the poor, amongst the poor and for the poor. This is not a poor church primarily on its way to becoming a middle class church, but a second form of being the people of God that has its own integrity and its own peculiar witness to the global church.[7]

- Missiological – the Liberation theologians do not move from abstract theological thinking to praxis. Instead, they move from the praxis of love of God and love of neighbour in service of the poor to theological reflection. Theology is, therefore, a second move, and not the first. The praxis of love and service is the first move and from this praxis a missional theology is constructed.

Clearly these themes pose a challenge to Evangelical thinking and mission. A challenge worth engaging so that our own Evangelical theology and praxis may be enriched and deepened and God's heart for the poor may find a deeper resonance in our lives.[8]

The way this chapter will unfold is as follows.

---

[7] While Pope Paul VI was very concerned that the Base Ecclesial Communities "remain firmly attached to the local Church," he nevertheless saw them as "hope for the universal Church" (Evangelii Nutiandi 1989, p. 68).

[8] I am in no way suggesting that the Liberation theologians cannot learn from Evangelicals. Evangelical clarity in presenting the gospel with its call to embrace the salvific work of God in Christ through the power of the Spirit is one challenge to the Liberation theologians. However, I am not suggesting they do not preach the gospel. L. and C. Boff (1987, p. 53) are clear: "Jesus, the Son of God, took on oppression to set us free."

- the Biblical basis for service to the poor will briefly and in summary form be set out;

- main themes of the church in its long history in serving the poor will be highlighted;

- the suggestion that Evangelicalism sees service to the poor as incidental and often peripheral, rather than central, will need to be clearly demonstrated;

- the above themes of the Liberation theologians will be set out in greater detail and depth; and

- the challenges that the Liberation theologians bring to Evangelicals will be set out, followed by a conclusion.

A comment needs to be made about the title of this chapter. This chapter is *not* based on the writings of Liberation theologians directly addressing Evangelicals. The Liberation theologians have tended to bring their main debate to bear on other Roman Catholic scholars and mainstream Protestant theologians. See, for example, Juan Luis Segundo who engages J. Moltmann, J. Metz, R. Niebuhr, and Ruben Alves amongst others (Segundo 1976, pp. 125-153). Interestingly a brief critique is given of C. Peter Wagner's writings (1975, pp. 134-135).

The dialogue in the other direction has not been very significant either. Vinay Samuel and Chris Sugden's extensive work: *Mission as Transformation: A Theology of the Whole Gospel* has only scant references to a number of Liberation theologians, and no extensive discussion and debate is found in its pages (Samuel & Sugden 1999, pp. 132; 164; 204).[9]

---

[9] There are some Evangelical scholars who form an exception and have engaged Liberation theology (Kirk 1985; Costas 1989; Langmead 2004).

So what this paper seeks to do is provide a fuller listening to the challenges that the Liberation theologians bring, particularly to us as Evangelicals,[10] as we pass through the windows of the Biblical narrative and the church's praxis in history.

A brief synopsis of the Biblical perspectives regarding the poor

The point that first and foremost needs to be made is that God's love and concern is for the *whole* of humanity (1Timothy 2:3-4; Titus 2:11). In fact, God's concern is for the whole created order and its full liberation (Romans 8:21) so that all things will find its full culmination in Christ (Colossians 1:20). Thus God desires the salvation of the Pharaohs of this world as well as those who have been oppressed by the powerful.[11]

The conversion of both to the heart and purposes of God has interesting and challenging implications. For the powerful, conversion involves moving into the purposes of God in caring for and in repentance regarding the poor. For the poor, conversion involves empowerment and forgiveness to oppressors. Clearly only a Kingdom of God theology can frame these transformational themes (Boff & Boff 1987, pp. 52-53; Snyder 1991).

Having said this, more needs to be said, namely, that the

---

[10] I recognise that the term 'Evangelical' is not without its problems. It can range from people holding a narrow fundamentalism through to more radical positions. I place myself in the broad Evangelical tradition well set out by my former colleague, Stanley Grenz (2000).

[11] While Martin Luther King Jr. believed that "we are called to speak for the weak, for the voiceless" (Ringma 2004, Reflection 112), he also emphasised that both the oppressed and the oppressor needed conversion and transformation. He writes, "we are all caught in an inescapable network of mutuality" (Washington 1991, p. 254). He went on to say that "God is interested in the freedom of the whole human race and in the creation of a society where all ... can live together ..." (p. 215).

Biblical story is awash with God's concern for the poor (Psalm 146:7-9) and the call to be like God in serving the poor (Deuteronomy 15:12-17). This vision enters most of the books of the Bible and, therefore, may not and should not be considered as incidental or peripheral.

While there are many important themes in the Biblical writings regarding the poor, and the Bible acknowledges that poverty may be self-inflicted due to laziness and other factors (Proverbs 10:4; 20:13), the major themes are those of love and mercy leading to charity and the work for justice on behalf of the poor. A further major theme is the problem of the oppression of the poor.[12] These themes need further elaboration.

Key terms

Charity

While the word *charity* is not a key word in the Bible regarding the poor, even though it is a key concept in the ministry of the church's service to the poor (Phan 1984, p. 20; Himmelfarb 1991, p. 6), the basic ideas in the notion of charity are everywhere present in the Bible, particularly when charity is seen as "provision of help or relief to the poor" based on "an act or feeling of benevolence, goodwill or affection" (*Reader's Digest Great Illustrated Dictionary*, 1984, 2 Vols, p. 301). The words "help" (Leviticus 25:35; 2 Corinthians 8:19, NIV),[13] "generosity" (Psalm 37:25-28; 2 Corinthians 9:5; 1 Timothy 6:18,

---

[12] The Bible does not speak about the poor without a range of meanings and nuances. The two most basic meanings are: (1) the poor in the sense of the humble who acknowledge their need for God (Psalm 34:6; 86:1); and (2) the economic and social poor (Leviticus 19:10; Deuteronomy 15:11). The focus of this paper is on the economic poor. However, this does not mean poor only in relation to finances. Poverty is much more comprehensive. Thus it also means poor in relation to such things as education, health, and opportunities.

[13] Scripture reference from the Holy Bible, NEW INTERNATIONAL VERSION®. Copyright © 1973, 1978, 1984 by Biblica, Inc. All rights reserved worldwide. Used by permission.

NIV), "give" (Deuteronomy 15:1-10; Matthew 6:2-3; Mark 10:21, NIV) are much more common, but they carry similar meanings to that of charity.

Justice

The word *justice* reoccurs much more frequently throughout the Biblical story. In many ways it is a much more powerful idea than that of charity. While charity is the expression of help to a person or persons in need of immediate help because of pressing need, justice is the more long term work of changing conditions of injustice, marginalisation or oppression so that people can live in circumstances that are equitable and fair. In other words, they can live God's *shalom* (Wright 1995, pp. 26-45). This fairness or justice comes from some norming standard. In general society, that is the law. In the Biblical story and in Christianity, that is God's vision of redemptive justice.

Martin Luther King, Jr. illustrates the difference between these two key words – charity and justice – helpfully, "we are called to play the Good Samaritan on life's roadside, but that will be only an initial act ... we must come to see that the whole Jericho road must be transformed so that men and women will not be constantly beaten and robbed as they make their journey on life's highway" (Ringma 2004, Reflection 43).

Because God loves justice (Psalm 37:28; Deuteronomy 32:4; Revelation 16:7) we are called to practise the work of justice on behalf of all and particularly the poor because justice is so often denied to them (Proverbs 21:3; Jeremiah 23:5; Deuteronomy 27:19; Ezekiel 22:29; Amos 2:7; Matthew 12:18; Luke 18:6-8).

This work of doing justice is helpfully and challengingly prefigured in the Old Testament concepts of Sabbath year, Jubilee and laws on gleaning and tithing (Sider 1980, pp. 78-83; Ringe 1985). It is also set out in a descriptive whole of life ethic (Ezekiel 18:5-9), the visionary dream of Isaiah (Isaiah 65:17-25), the ethics and practice of Jesus (Luke 6:20; 7:22-23; 14:15-24), the theological concept of oneness in Christ (Galatians 3:28-29; 1 Corinthians 12:12-13), the idea that there may be "equality" (NIV) or "a fair balance" (NRSV) (2 Corinthians 8:12-14), and finally the practice of care for the poor is set out in the General Epistles (James 2:1-7).[14]

If matters concerning the poor were only cast in terms of their vices or bad luck or social conditioning or the national or global economy, the issue of poverty could more easily be relegated to the sidelines. And we need to admit that we have a tendency to do this. We often put the poor and issues of poverty in some convenient explanatory box.[15] The box is often a dismissive one, or worse, one of sheer indifference and neglect.

Oppression

The Biblical story, however, does not allow us to dwell there, for the poor are most basically also the subject of some form of *oppression*. And if there is anything that is writ large in the Bible's pages, it is that it knows the language of oppression

---

[14] The Evangelical scholar, Waldron Scott, has made a powerful plea that mission cannot be understood simply in terms of the Great Commission. Mission, he says, has to do with rectification (Scott 1980, p. xv) and this involves the central Biblical motif of the establishment of justice (p. xvi).

[15] At the beginning of teaching the Urban Anthropology and Mission course at Asian Theological Seminary in the 1990's students were asked to find words and images that expressed their attitudes toward the poor. Most words were negative. At the end of the semester, after students had done significant fieldwork in a slum or urban poor community, their language regarding the poor had changed and many positive words were used to describe the poor.

and injustice with its consequences of marginalisation, neglect, empoverishment and disempowerment (Tamez 1982).[16]

The Lord is "a stronghold for the oppressed" (Psalm 9:9); wants no one to be oppressed (Psalm 104:12); and "executes justice for the oppressed" (Psalm 146:7). We are therefore called to join the God of justice and to cease from all forms of oppression. And, positively, as we have seen, we are to practise helpfulness and justice to bring others into God's shalom.

The Bible in its sheer realism recognises that oppression will occur. Isaiah expresses this most succinctly, "people will be oppressed" (Isaiah 3:5). This leads to affliction and misery (Psalm 44:24), and as a result people cry out under an oppressive load (Job 35:9) looking to Yahweh to come to their aid (Psalm 119:134).

While oppression in the Biblical story takes many forms, economic as well as military and political (2 Kings 13:22; Isaiah 52:4), our focus here is oppression in relation to the poor. What is clear is that the powerful oppress the poor and exploit them. Isaiah is brutal in his observation "the spoil of the poor is in your houses" (Isaiah 4:14). Moreover, the poor are deprived of their rights (Proverbs 31:5) and are pushed aside by the powerful (Amos 5:12).

The driving problem with oppression is that it tends to be compounded resulting in multiple difficulties for the poor thus making poverty a most disempowering issue. Conrad Boerma

---

[16] Tamez (1982) has been particularly helpful in drawing attention to the compound meanings carried by some of the key OT words for oppression - nagash, anah, lahats. Beside the core meanings of oppression and exploitation, further shades of meaning include: to degrade, subdue, violate another, harass, and to drive someone in a corner (Exodus 5:10, 13, 14; 1:11; 3:7,9).

points this out in the Old Testament witness. When you have traders who exploit the poor (Hosea 12:7-8; Amos 8:5-6; Micah 6:10-12), corrupt judges (Amos 5:7; Micah 3:9-11; Isaiah 5:23), and the seizure of your wages, goods, property or land (Isaiah 4:14; Jer 22:13; Micah 2:2; Ezekiel 22:29), then you create a setting where the poor have no one to turn to and you have instituted the politics of despair (Boerma, 1979).

The vision of redemption

This oppression of the poor is not that of the stranger or foreigner against the people of God, but Israeli oppressing Israeli. This violates the most fundamental theme of the entire Biblical story. For not only should we not oppress and exploit others, because they too are created in the image of God, but we should not oppress others because we have been delivered by God from oppression in order to bless others. In other words, by oppressing others we violate the very foundation of God's *redemptive activity*, for the freedom that God has extended to us by his grace is a freedom also for others.

The Old Testament Liberation scholar J. Severino Croatto is possibly the most helpful in spelling out the fundamental nature of redemption and deliverance and how this is diametrically opposed to all forms of oppression whether political, social, economic, or gender.

Just as redemption through Christ is the central motif of the New Testament, so the Exodus event with its liberation of the Hebrew slaves in Egypt is key to the Old Testament narrative. Croatto points out that the Exodus event is both a spiritual and social reality in that the discouraged Hebrews were re-vitalised and they were freed from their captivity and oppression. The Exodus event, therefore, involves Passover (Exodus 12), worship (Exodus 3:12; 5:3,8), and real deliverance of a people. In other words, God's redemptive activity is not simply inward renewal. It is also communal freedom (Croatto 1981).

This redemptive event has significant flow-on effects. In fact, it is foundational and paradigmatic, for the Exodus deliverance becomes the central confession of Israel's faith, life and identity (Deuteronomy 26:5-8) and the defining characteristic of Israel's life (Psalm 80:8; 105:23-45; 106:21-22; 114:1; 135:8; 136:13-15). In other words, the Israelites are a chosen and redeemed people and this marks them to be a blessing for others, for redemption pulls a people into the slipstream of the purposes of God for the whole of humanity and the world.

Furthermore, the deliverance of the Israelites becomes normative ethically. Living God's redemption is to act redemptively. Thus the Israelites were to extend Exodus to others – both to their own people who were among them, but in difficulty and hardship, and to the sojourner and stranger (Deuteronomy 15:12-17; 24:17-22). The key motif is, "you shall not deprive a resident alien or an orphan of justice ... Remember that you were a slave in Egypt and the Lord redeemed you ..." (Deuteronomy 27:17-18).

This motif regarding the practical outworking of our redemption is key to the New Testament. The Nazareth Manifesto (Luke 4:18-19) is not only the charter for how God in Christ acts redemptively towards those seeking salvation, but becomes normative for the redeemed to act towards others (Luke 6:27-36). Little wonder then that Matthew makes a direct connection between service to the poor as a way of serving

Christ (Matthew 25:34-46). The New Testament Epistles emphasise not only that if we are in Christ we are linked to our brothers and sisters in Christ (1 Corinthians 12:12-13), but that the slave or poor person is now a brother (Philemon 1:16; Galatians 3:27-29) and should be regarded and treated accordingly (James 2:1-7). The simple reality of this is almost mundanely expressed by Paul, "Thieves must give up stealing; rather let them labour and work honestly with their own hands, *so as* to have something to share with the needy" (Ephesians 4:28, my emphasis).

Conclusion

The Biblical story's concern about the poor and their oppression and the call to practice justice, kindness and humility (Micah 6:8) is central to its ethos because it is rooted in the nature of redemption. This is so because redemption is both a relational concept and it has vertical and horizontal dimensions. Redemption has profound social implications.

Redemption is not packaged. It is a transformational reality. Drawn to God, redemption is God's gift of renewal, healing and freedom. This is the vertical dimension. But this God calls the redeemed into God's service for the blessing of humanity, and humanity is *never* well blessed if the least are on the scrap heap of our global economy and on the garbage dumps of our wastefulness. Instead, when the least, the poor, the marginalised are served well then the God of justice dances with delight.

The church in its long history in serving the poor

Given that the section above sets out something of the Biblical vision regarding God's concern for the poor, it should not surprise us that the church throughout its long journey has sought to live that out, albeit in times of radical faithfulness, as well as in seasons of disappointing compromise and neglect.

While this story – as well as that of the Biblical story – is too extensive to set out in this limited space, there are a number of things that I wish to do in giving some of its main contours. First, I wish to demonstrate the nature and scope of the church's service to the poor. In other words, what did Christians actually *do* in serving the poor. Second, what are some of the factors in the fluctuations that occurred in serving the poor, and what can we learn from the times of triumph and of neglect. Third, how does this long journey reflect the Biblical narrative and provide hope for our present journey in serving the poor.

It is possible to set out many epochs in tracing this journey of the church. For the sake of brevity we will look at the pre-Constantinian period, the church in the post-Constantinian era, the church in the Middle Ages, the Reformation churches and beyond, and the church in the modern world.

The pre-Constantinian church

A number of preliminary comments should be made before setting out the major contours of the church's service in this period from the New Testament and the church in persecution to the church as part of Constantine's empire. The most basic is the warning not to over idealise the church in this period. The church of Early Christianity was young and vital, but also messy and it was greatly challenged to live out its radical vision of a new people in Christ, especially in relation to slavery. Furthermore, it also needs to be realised that the church in this period was an absolute marginal minority movement within the Roman Empire. There were probably some 200,000 Christians in a Roman world of some 30 million. This severely limited what they could do regarding an impact on society.

From the writings of the Early Church Fathers the main themes of response to the poor are clear.

- Money was raised through almsgiving and this was distributed by deacons.
- The most basic impetus was to care for the needy within the faith community. This included attempts to buy the freedom of Christians condemned to prison or to work in mines as slaves.
- In settings of natural or social or political disaster or other crises, Christians extended practical help to others. This included paying for burial services of strangers.
- Christians practised hospitality to strangers. However, this was mainly extended to brothers and sisters in the faith.
- Some Christian churches used church funds to buy the freedom of slaves (Phan 1984, pp. 20-23).
- The Early Church Father, Tertullian observes, "Our care for the derelict and our active love have become our distinctive sign before the enemy" (Phan 1984, p. 21). This active love included bringing up the children of prostitutes and gladiators and infants who were abandoned on the rubbish dumps of cities in the Roman Empire (Oliver 1930, p. 31).

Ignatius, in setting out the duties of presbyters, commented that they had the responsibility of "caring for all the weak, neglecting neither widow, nor orphan nor poor" (Oliver 1930, p. 32). To make that specific Bishop Cornelius in 250 AD wrote, "The Roman church supports 1500 widows and poor persons" (Harnack 1962, p. 159). We learn of these acts of charity not only from voices *within* the Christian church but also from outsiders. Julian the Apostate wrote, "These godless Galileans feed not only their own poor, but ours [as well]; our poor lack care" (Harnack, p. 162).

This first chapter, then, in the church's long march in history demonstrates that Christians both cared for the weak and poor in their own midst, but also extended that concern to others primarily in acts of kindness, helpfulness and care, or the praxis of charity. As Troeltsch summarises, this was not so much the Early Church trying to change the world and create "a new social order" (1960, Vol. I, p. 135). Instead, it was the "awakening of the spirit of love ... which Christ imparts" (p. 134). As such it "was simply and solely the work of charity" (p. 134). This was the church's way "of healing social wounds" and according to Troeltsch this "constitutes a brilliant chapter in ... [the church's] history" (p. 134).

The Constantinian and post-Constantinian church

In this period the marginal and persecuted church becomes the church of the Empire, which gains it the support of the State and its resultant respectability and influence. This is the time that the church becomes highly organised and much of its response to the poor and needy and to society in general takes the form of the creation of more *institutional* forms of care.

In summary we note the following developments.

- From hospices, the first hospitals are established in the 4th century.
- Monastic communities are established which extended hospitality and care for the poor, and developed farming practices.
- Schools were established.
- Gladiatorial events were suppressed.
- Women gained more rights.
- While slavery continued, slaves were bought their freedom.
- Prisoners of war were also bought their freedom. Ambrose, bishop of Milan "sold rich church ornaments to ransom captives who had fallen into the hands of the Goths" (Oliver 1930, p. 66).
- Churches continued to care for thousands of poor in their respective cities (Oliver 1930, pp. 45-77).

While charity continued in this period the church, with much greater social influence, was able to address general social concerns (e.g. gladiatorial events) as well as create many general social institutions (e.g. schools and hospitals) which provided services of care to people in need in the general society.

Service to the poor in the Middle Ages

This period of the church in history witnessed the attempt of a great synthesis between church and state and church and society based on a theological vision. In the words of Troeltsch, the Middle Ages "witnessed the expansion of the church to a comprehensive, unifying, and reconciling social whole, which included both the sociological circle of religion itself and the politico-social organisations" (1960, Vol. I, p. 203). This interpenetration of church and state meant, not simply a more powerful role for the church in society, but also that the church was drawn more and more into other areas of social concern. Thus bishops played not only a role in religious matters but also "civic and penal legislation" (p. 211).

In this period the church itself became a rich landowner. This also was true of the monastic orders. This time in the church's life saw some helpful developments in the church's role in society, but there were also many concerns.

The more helpful developments may be summarised as follows.

- There continued to be a great emphasis on almsgiving and the practice of charity. The church devoted one third of its income to poor relief (Oliver 1930, p. 101).

- The church because of its power and influence was able to be a great civilising force in society.

- The merchant and trade gilds of this time constituted a form "of lay charity and social service" in that they helped bury "the dead, gave dowries to poor girls and rendered other social services" (p. 99).

- The laws of the land began to reflect general Christian values, thus "law and legal penalty" was substituted "for private revenge" (p. 98).

- The flourishing of art, the building of cathedrals, the

writing and producing of books gave a richness to life (pp. 94-96).

However, there were many concerns that reflected negatively on the way the church went about doing good.

- Almsgiving and the practice of charity became loaded with special spiritual significance so that it accrued merit for the giver (Oliver 1930, p. 103).

- With the giver, rather than the recipient being the focus of attention and with impulsive giving in order to receive grace, poverty was fed rather than alleviated (p. 104).

- With an emphasis on natural law and patriarchalism a set of values was engendered that promoted social conservatism and stability and the idea of gratitude to benefactors which created greater dependencies. "The continual exhortations to the lower classes to evince humility and gratitude, and to the ruling classes to exercise care and love" (Troeltsch 1960, Vol. I, p. 286), "corrupted both the givers and the receivers" (Oliver 1930, p. 105).

This synthesis of church and state and law and grace attempted to create an organic whole that lacked self-critical impulses. But the critique came anyway in the form of 'sectarian' movements which included the Waldensians, the Franciscans, the Lollards, the Hussites and the Moravians (Troeltsch 1960, Vol. I, pp. 349-369). These interestingly enough sought their inspiration for serving the poor in the vision and ethos of Early Christianity. This highlights the more general observation that in times of renewal the move of the church in history is to find inspiration from the Biblical story and the ethos of Early Christianity, rather than from its current practices.

The Reformation and beyond

While the church in the Middle Ages shaped by the integral theological vision of Thomas Aquinas sought to create a Christian society, the Reformation brought with it a new sense of direction.

Though some attempts were made at the older synthesis (e.g. Calvin's Geneva) and there was co-operation between church and state (e.g. Luther and the German princes), the Reformation vision was much more that of a renewed and revitalised church making an impact on society through its church related institutions and the role of the laity in the society.

However the huge task in renewing the church, theology, liturgy and other aspects of the church's life, as well as the significant changes occurring in society, the wars of religion and eventually the spawning of an arid Protestant orthodoxy, led to a lack of a missional and societal impetus. Furthermore, with more democratic impulses in the society general laws were passed that had the poor in view. Oliver thus notes that the "tendency in Protestant countries was to leave the care of the poor to the state" (Oliver 1930, p. 117). That good works no longer held special merit must also be held responsible for a lapse "of zeal in social work" (p. 116).

Nevertheless, the Reformation emphasis on grace, the importance of the individual, a renewed community of faith, and the role of the state, did lead to new ideas and practices regarding the poor and needy. In summary the more important emphases should be noted.

- The good of the recipient, not the giver, must be the primary focus, and assistance should be evaluated in terms of effectiveness.
- Only the worthy should be helped. The unfortunate and helpless, not the lazy, should be assisted.
- Aid should be focused to solve particular needs and problems. In other words, the focus should be to create long term solutions.
- Support *systems* need to be put in place to sustain worthy projects.
- Policy needs to be developed in the doing of social work.
- Civil authorities need to play their part in helping the poor (Oliver 1930, p. 115).

The above practices reflect an important shift from the Middle Ages and begin to prefigure some of the practices of the Modern World. As in the Middle Ages it was the renewal movements within Protestantism (e.g. the Methodists) that carried forward much of the vision in helping the poor and in seeking to change aspects of society (Hyson 1984; Snyder 1980; Hempton 1996).

Troeltsch in his long discussion of Protestantism (1960, Vol. II, pp. 461-820), and in particular its Calvinistic variant which he calls ascetic Protestantism (p. 808), summarises this tradition in terms of "unceasing ... labor," "the habit of industry to suppress all distracting and idle impulses and the willingness to use "profit for the religious community and for public welfare" (pp. 808-809). What this means is that the basic ethic was that those with resources were to be generous. But there was little sense of notions of radical identification with the poor. Moreover the charity, rather than the social justice model, continued to predominate.

Serving the poor in the Modern World

Global poverty and injustice

While each of the time periods, which we have somewhat arbitrarily designated, constitutes both continuity in ways of serving the poor, as well as changes, the transition to our day constitutes the most significant change. In case some of the readers may wish for some of the gaps to be filled in for the period from the Reformation to the present, I suggest Bosch's treatment of mission in the wake of the Enlightenment (Bosch 1991, pp. 262-345).

There are many factors that have contributed to where we are now in the contemporary world, including the development of post-colonial states in the Third world or Majority world, factors of globalisation and issues of climate change. My focus, however, will be on some factors in global Christianity and world poverty.

The map of world Christianity has radically changed. In the post-Reformation world Christianity was largely Western. Today 70% of Christians are in the Third World (Laing 2006). Since many of these countries struggle with issues of poverty and many Christians are actually poor, the issue of poverty has come to rest (and agitate) within the *bosom* of the church itself. The church is thus not only concerned about the poor, but the church itself is a church *of* the poor. This calls the church to a new sense of self-identity, theology and praxis.

The map of world poverty is huge in its spread and fraught with challenges. In a world of some 6.7 billion people, nearly three billion live on less than $2 per day and one billion people are chronically malnourished resulting in an annual death of 40 million people, including children as the majority, who die of starvation and related but preventable illnesses.

This map is also framed by global injustice. The world's 20% of the population living in developed economies consume 80% of the world's goods. One needs little imagination to think of where that leaves the rest of the world. To make that more specific: the richest 50 million persons in the First World have the same combined income as 2.7 billion poor in the Majority World. But of course there is much more to this complex story. It is not simply a matter of the Minority World exploiting the rest of humanity. The Third World's fragile economies, unstable governments, and military dictatorships continue to harass and exploit their own people. We need only think of the current tragic situation in Zimbabwe.

In case you think that things are getting better and fairer, this appears not to be the case. In 1960, 20% of the world population living in the First World had 30 times the income of the poorest 20%. In 2000 the well-to-do had 80 times more. And in 2001, 497 billionaires registered a combined income of US$1.54 trillion. This is equivalent to the combined income of the poorest half of humanity. This while the First World spends US$12 billion annually on perfumes and US$17 billion on pet food.

If this is not bad enough please register the fact that the Majority World spends US$13 on debt repayment for every US$1 it receives in development grants.[17]

What this means is that not only is a sizeable proportion of global Christianity poor, but global Christians live in a world of dire poverty and gross injustice. These issues are well beyond the challenges that faced the church in earlier epochs.

In the light of the above, we may now ask the question, how are contemporary Christians responding to these challenges? In order to summarise much of the key thinking regarding these issues I will turn to Roman Catholic Social Teaching (Henriot 1992), key texts from the Ecumenical Movement (Kinnamon & Cope 1997) and the missional documents from the Lausanne Movement (Stott 1997). We will begin with the last first.

The Evangelical movement

Of the nine major missional documents from the Lausanne Movement, it is the 1982 Grand Rapids Report on Evangelism and Social Responsibility (Stott 1997, pp. 165-213) that deals most explicitly with service to the poor. In the other documents ministry to the poor is not a focus or it is fairly marginal with only occasional references (Stott 1997, pp. 24, 34, 90, 92, 102, 105, 145, 146, 147, 162). The primal 1974 Lausanne Covenant does state, "We, therefore, should share his (God's) concern for justice and reconciliation throughout human society and for the liberation of men from every kind of oppression" (p. 24). But this theme is not sustained throughout the document. The only exception to

---

[17] These statistics were accessed on http://www.Globalissues.org

the more extensive Grand Rapids Report is the Manila Manifesto (Stott 1997, pp. 225-249).

In the Manila Manifesto reference is made to the fact that God's concern for the poor is spoken about in the "law, the prophets and the wisdom books, and the teaching and ministry of Jesus" (Stott 1997, p. 234). It also contains a call to repentance "where we have been indifferent to the plight of the poor" (p. 235). It then makes reference to the importance of word and deed in ministry and the call "to preach and teach, minister to the sick, feed the hungry, care for prisoners, help the disadvantaged and handicapped and deliver the oppressed" (p. 236).

However, the overall focus of the document is on world evangelisation in the light of the fact that over two billion people have not heard the gospel (p. 245).

The main argument in the Grand Rapids Report is that while "evangelism has a certain priority" (Stott 1997, p. 183) "social activity is a *consequence* of evangelism" (p. 111). It goes on to argue that social concern is also "a *bridge* to evangelism" (p. 181) and is "its *partner*" (p. 182).

However, the Report does not carry us forward beyond this. It talks briefly about philanthropic service and development (Stott 1997, p. 197), the role of the local church to be socially concerned (p. 198) and must raise a prophetic voice about justice issues (p. 203) and for Western Christians to adopt a simple lifestyle (p. 206). It concludes with a reference to individual Biblical characters who defied "human authority in the name of the God of justice" (p. 208).

In the next major section I will evaluate this material, but the overall picture is fairly clear. These evangelical documents prioritise the work of evangelism and recognise the need for social concern, but the documents are skimpy in articulating a vision and strategies for this concern. There is no in-depth Biblical discussion and no strategic vision that implements a concern for the poor. The words regarding the poor 'hang in the air'. There are no strategies to wash the feet of the world. Thus service to the poor remains secondary and peripheral.

The Ecumenical movement

The documents in Kinnamon & Cope's anthology (1997) deal with the unity of the church, issues of division among the churches, dialogue with people of other faiths, councils of the churches, prayer and worship and regional voices of churches in the Majority World. Amongst these are two other sets of documents. The one is on ecumenical social thought (pp. 263-324) and the other deals with mission and evangelism (pp. 325-392).

In the latter set of documents there is an emphasis on *kerygma*: the gospel proclaimed, *koinonia*: the gospel lived in community, and *diakonia*: the gospel demonstrated in service (Kinnamon & Cope 1997, p. 336). And in the famous International Missionary Council (Willingen, Germany 1952) the concept of *missio Dei* was set out, namely, that mission is following the Triune missional God into the world (p. 339). This is done within a Kingdom of God theology (p. 340) and involves the church's incarnational presence in the world: "The church is required to identify itself with the world, not only in its perplexity and distress, its guilt and sorrow, but also in its real acts of love and justice" (p. 341).

The theological framework above provides the basis for a call in 1968 to reach the poor (Kinnamon & Cope 1997, p. 347). This was more fully set out in the 1973 Bangkok conference which emphasised that the salvation of Christ "offers a comprehensive wholeness in this divided life" (p. 356) and this salvation involves us "in the struggle for economic justice against exploitation" (p. 357).

However, it is the 1982 World Council of Churches (WCC) Commission on World Mission and Evangelism that most clearly sets out the mission of the church to the poor. The document states that many of the world's poor suffer a double loss: they have not heard the gospel and they are the victims of oppression (Kinnamon & Cope 1997, p. 378). Therefore the church should live a "preferential option for the poor" (p. 379). This means the poor should be made a priority. It goes on to say that a "proclamation that does not hold forth the promises of the justice of the Kingdom to the poor of the earth is a caricature of the gospel" (p. 379).

This document also states that the poor can evangelise us. "God is working through the poor of the earth to awaken the consciousness of humanity to his call for repentance, for justice and for love" (Kinnamon & Cope 1997, p. 380).

Most of the documents dealing with Ecumenical Social Thought address broader issues of the church in society, the role of the state, racism and economics, but there are references to the poor. The 1954 WCC Assembly in Evanston summarises: "The Churches have a duty to promote adequate assistance on the national and international level for children, the sick, the old, refugees, and other economically weak groups" (Kinnamon &

Cope 1997, p. 287).

The World Conference on church and society in Geneva, 1966, encourages the churches to help Third World countries in their economic development (Kinnamon & Cope 1997, p. 292), it calls the church to discern what God is doing in the change and protest movements among the poor (p. 297) and calls the church to a prophetic role in society (pp. 297-298).

The Boston conference of 1979 calls the church to help build a "just, participatory and sustainable society" (Kinnamon & Cope 1997, p. 305) while at the same time recognising that the church in its own life must demonstrate this justice as a faith community (p. 313). This is followed up in the Larnaca conference of 1986, which recognises the church's complicity in oppression. It reads, "We confess our sin and confess our complicity in upholding ... structures and systems in the churches and society that oppress human beings" (p. 315). It then refers to global trade arrangements that discriminate against the Third World (p. 316).

Finally, in the Seoul 1990 conference reference is made to the poor's need for fullness of life (John 10:10) and for justice. It articulates God's preferential option for the poor (p. 318) and argues that charity and aid are not enough. More fundamental changes are necessary for "a just, equitable world economic order" (Kinnamon & Cope 1997, p. 319).

These perspectives constitute a significant emphasis on a response to the poor. Rooted in Biblical concepts and in a Trinitarian and Kingdom theology these conferences recognise the need for personal and structural change in relation to the poor. With articulating God's preferential option for the poor, these documents argue for a centrality and priority in serving the poor.

Roman Catholic social teaching

Pope Leo's XIII 1891 *Rerum Novarum* which explores the role of the church in society and the duties of employers and workers, highlights the need for public authorities to protect the rights of the poor and the need for help, care and support for the poor (Henriot 1992, p. 31). This emphasis is picked up again by Pope Pius XI in his 1931 *Quadragesimo Anno* which calls for just wages and is very concerned about the way in which workers are exploited (p. 36). This theme of just wages is also a theme in Pope John's XXIII 1961 *Mater et Magistra* (p. 40). The culmination of this earlier period of Roman Catholic Social Documents is *Gaudium et Spes*, 1965, one of the key documents of the Second Vatican Council. The document highlights the discrepancies between the First World and the Third World (Flannery 1996, p. 166), the cry of poor for justice (p. 170), what is necessary to live "a genuinely human life" (p. 191), and the call of the church to act on behalf of the needy (p. 210). The document laments that often economic progress is at the expense of the poor (p. 242) and does not benefit all in a society (p. 243). It concludes: "God destined the earth and all it contains for all people and nations so that all created things would be shared fairly by all humankind under the guidance of justice tempered by charity" (p. 248).

The 1971 Statement of the Synod of Bishops, *Justice in the World* promotes the idea that "action on behalf of justice and participation in the transformation of the world fully appear to us as a constitutive dimension of the preaching of the gospel" (Henriot 1992, p. 64). The 1975 *Evangelii Nuntiandi* of Pope Paul VI holds that "evangelization has a personal and social dimension involving human rights, peace, justice, development and liberation" (p. 69).

Moving to regional areas the Latin American Medellin conference of 1968 voiced that Jesus was "liberator from sin, hunger, oppression, misery [and] ignorance" (Henriot 1992, p. 127), argued for structural justice (p. 129) and articulated strategies of empowerment and conscientization (p. 128). The Puebla conference in 1979 spoke of political repression, abuse of political power and the violation of human rights (p. 131) and calls the church to "a radical discipleship and a love that gives a privileged place to the poor" (p. 132). This is formulated as God's preferential option for the poor (p. 133). This commitment calls "for conversion on the part of the whole church" (Hennelly 1990, p. 254); it is a following of Christ whose mission was directed to the poor (p. 255); calls the church to "evangelical poverty" by being in solidarity with the poor (pp. 256-257); and at its heart involves the proclamation of "Christ the saviour" (p. 256) and working to change "unjust social, political and economic structures" (p. 257).

These emphases, including the option for the poor, are also articulated in Pope John Paul's II *Sollicitudo Rei Socialis* of 1988. This document suggests that the whole church tradition bears witness to "love of preference for the poor" (Henriot 1992, p. 82), calls for solidarity between the rich and poor (p. 77), and challenges the church to concern itself with development issues (p. 80).

John Paul's II subsequent *Redemptoris Missio*, 1990, following the above themes suggests that the "Church is called to be on the side of the poor and oppressed" (Henriot 1992, p. 87) even though the "Kingdom is meant for all humankind" and "Christ is the one savior of all" (p. 85).

These Roman Catholic documents argue for a profound commitment of personal change in Christ, the conversion of the church to the side of the poor as a way of following Christ, and for engaging the world for its transformation. Here the documents see the need to overcome injustice and structural evil through practices that promote *shalom*. Clearly in these documents God's concern for the poor and our participation in that concern is seen as central.

Conclusion

This journey of looking at the church's praxis in serving the poor over two thousand years highlights the church's fundamental commitment to serve the poor. This vision, though it has fluctuated, has never been completely lost. This means that the tradition of the church underscores the Biblical vision that the God who is concerned for the poor and who is a God of justice, is a God we are called to follow.

The articulation of this history serves a number of purposes in this essay.

- It highlights the importance of service to the poor.
- It suggests that this is central to being Godlike and to the *imitatio Christi*.
- It anticipates that much of what the liberation theologians have articulated regarding service to the poor fits

- It gives us a basis for evaluating the evangelical tradition.

Critiquing the evangelical tradition in relation to serving the poor

There are a number of preliminary comments that must be made. The first is that this is my tradition, so what I am saying by way of critique also applies to me.[18] In fact, I feel quite unhappy about the way my involvement with and my response to the poor has unfolded. Secondly, I recognise that there are many Evangelicals who have developed both an adequate theology in relation to the poor and have demonstrated a praxis that accords with their theological vision. One need only think of Ronald Sider (1980, 1993, 1999) and John Perkins (1976, 1995) in the US, the late Athol Gill in Australia (1989, 1990, Pidwell 2007), Vinay Samuel in India, David Lim in the Philippines and R. Padilla in Argentina (Ringma 1998, p. 22). Thus my concern is not with individual Evangelicals but with the movement as a whole as represented in the Lausanne documents (Stott 1997).

As we have seen, the Lausanne documents deal with serving the poor and the Grand Rapids Report, 1982, is the most explicit about evangelism and social responsibility. However, I have major concerns, which may be itemised as follows.

- No report contains even a basic discussion of the Biblical vision of service to the poor. References to serving the poor are isolated. There is no cohesive Biblical framework.

---

[18] See my *Seek the Silences with Thomas Merton* where I have attempted some critique of my Reformed and Evangelical heritage (Ringma 2003).

- There is no sense of history in these documents. It is almost as if contemporary Evangelicals think that they are the first ones thinking about these matters. There is no reference to the Early Church Fathers, the Reformation or the Wesleyan revival.

- There is no dialogue with other church traditions. Evangelicals appear to be thinking about these matters by themselves. Yet, as we have seen, there is not only a rich Biblical vision but also a rich church tradition.

- Much of the discussion in these documents is bounded by the debate about the relationship between evangelism and social concern. With evangelism being identified as primary, the documents set up a dichotomous and dualistic way of thinking which will always leave social concern in a secondary place with the possible consequences of marginalisation and neglect. Evangelicals cannot seem to say that Jesus preached a gospel for the poor (Luke 7:22-23).

- It is most unfortunate that in the discussion of the Kingdom of God in the Grand Rapids Report no no reference is made to the poor (Stott 1997, pp. 186-190) when Luke, for example, makes a direct connection (Luke 4:18-19; 6:20).

- Evangelicalism has a tendency to neglect its historical memory and has ideas about a good God and the good life leading many of its adherents to a middle class mediocrity. Sider speaks of the US$8 billion spent by Evangelicals in the US on weight-reduction programs and US$2 billion spent of missions (Sider 1993, p. 191). Ideas of downward mobility and identification with the poor would be regarded as strange ideas given these middle class values.

- Given its evangelistic orientation, evangelicalism has a tendency to emphasise the spiritual dimensions of life, while the world of the poor is about putting food on the table, clean water, health issues, rural and urban migration, economics, politics and global trading realities. Not much of this world, apart from numbers of needing evangelisation, is reflected in the Lausanne documents.

- The Lausanne documents reflect little on a critique of the principalities and powers, the nature of structural evil, false ideologies and oppressive global arrangements and so on. Thus there is something naïve about its analysis and this has implications for the movement's missional response to the poor. If structural analysis is weak, then strategies may well be simplistic.

- Finally, Evangelicals, like their heroes in Western movies, tend to think of individual heroes. It celebrates such people. But this does not mean that the commitment to identification with the poor is intrinsic to evangelical theology, the church and its missional practice.[19]

In the light of the above there is a threefold conclusion.

---

[19] See my *Cry Freedom with voices from the Third World* for other Evangelicals with a commitment to serve the poor (Ringma 1998) and see Ross Langmead's *The Word Made Flesh: Towards an Incarnational Missiology* for a list of what he calls "radical evangelicals" (Langmead 2004, p. 94).

- In the light of Biblical vision Evangelicals need to make their vision of serving the poor more central to their theology, church life and their missional practice.

- Evangelicals need to appropriate the long history of church and be more dialogical in their engagement with other church and theological traditions.

- As we shall see Evangelicals can learn from the Liberation theologians by taking mission to poor more central to their theology and praxis.

The voice of the Liberation theologians

I have already explained that this is not an attempt to defend all that the Liberation theologians have said and done. It is much more limited. I merely wish to draw on a number of important themes and emphases in Liberation theology regarding the poor that we can appropriate for our own evangelical tradition.

A hermeneutical reading of the Bible regarding the poor

There are many ways to read the Bible. One can do so from a historical-critical or a feminist perspective. These are two scholarly approaches. But as we shall see, there are many other differing approaches. There are also more naïve ways of reading the Biblical story. One could read the Bible as a book of comfort or as a book about the afterlife or heaven.

This raises the question whether these different ways of reading Scripture are equally helpful. Rudolf Bultmann thinks not. He suggests that psychological and historical ways of reading the text (that lock the text into the past) are less helpful ways of engaging Scripture. Instead, Bultmann opts for an "existential" reading. By this he means that one must have a life-relation to the text (Ringma 1999, p. 116) and that one must allow oneself to be confronted by the claims of the text (p. 153) which then leads to the possibility that I "could gain *a new understanding of myself from it*" (p. 153). In other words, Bultmann suggests that one should read and engage Scripture from a *transformational* perspective (Wink 1973).

The Liberation theologians clearly fit into a transformational reading of Scripture paradigm, but with a very particular slant. They read the Bible from "the underside of history (Gutierrez 1983, p. xi), or as Clodovis Boff puts it more specifically, the strategy is "To interrogate the totality of Scripture from the viewpoint of the oppressed" (Ellacuria & Sobrino 1993, p. 79). Boff goes on to say that "this is not the only possible legitimate reading of the Bible" (p. 79) but it is "the most *appropriate*" reading for the poor given their marginalisation and oppression (p. 79).

The Liberation theologians thus explore the great themes of Scripture in relation to the poor, which we have set out in the earlier part of this essay. Boff notes that these themes have to do with God as the Father of life and advocate of the oppressed; the exodus deliverance; the prophetic vision of a world full of shalom and justice; and the Reign of God for the poor in the mission of Jesus (Ellacuria & Sobrino 1993, p. 79).

The poor themselves also read the Bible in this way. "The poor look into the Bible for a truth that will set them free"

(Ellacuria & Sobrino 1993, p. 124)[20]. Thus like the theologians, the poor read the Bible from a committed point of view. This committed reading is that the God of the Bible is the God of Life who offers life and this God is the God of justice who offers liberation and freedom (pp. 124-125)[21].

The third grouping of people who read the Bible in this way is the 'evangelical poor'. These are Christians who move to the side of the poor, identifying with them and advocating on their behalf. The famous Puebla conference in Mexico in 1979 addressed this grouping. It first of all acknowledged that many religious orders (e.g. the Franciscans) were committed to serving the poor and identifying with them in their struggle for life (Hennelly 1990, p. 256). It goes on to say that "this model of the poor life is one that the gospel requires of all those who believe in Christ" (p. 256), including people from "the middle class" (p. 256). This commitment is not forced upon people but is "done out of love" (p. 256).

Finally, this hermeneutic, that is, this way of reading the Bible with all its transformational consequences, not only for the poor, but also for theologians (in doing their theology) and for middle class Christians (in committing to downward mobility), has further implications. The main theme is that the poor *themselves* become a text and need to be read and listened to. What this means is that as the Reign of God with its transformational and liberation power breaks in among the poor, the poor then become a witness, an embodiment of the gospel, and need to be read. The poor thus, in a secondary sense, become 'gospel'

---

[20] Little wonder that Viv Grigg argued for the need of movements among the poor rather than only heroic individuals (Grigg 1984, pp. 169).

[21] For the voice of the poor in discussing the gospels see Cardenal, 1982.

to us. They evangelise us. They demonstrate the love and power of the God of justice.[22]

Major themes in Liberation theology

Liberation theology is not a partial or truncated theology. It is a full-orbed theology, but from the perspective of the poor (Ellacuria & Sobrino 1993; Boff & Boff 1987). It sets out all the major themes of theology including Trinity, Kingdom of God, Christology, ecclesiology, the person and work of the Holy Spirit and eschatology. For a brief overview see Boff & Boff 1987, pp. 43-65, and for a much more extended theological articulation see Ellacuria & Sobrino, 1993.

This theology arose in South America because the "circumstances were ripe in Latin America" (Ellacuria & Sobrino 1993, p. 103). The social teaching of the church (which we have earlier traced) lay a foundation for this new theology (p. 104) and a new 'church' began to emerge in the form of the Base Ecclesial Communities. This was "a decentralized church ... in the service of the world and in solidarity with the poor and their cause" (pp. 198-199). This was the church of the poor among the poor which "connotes a church in which laity and religious, priests and bishops, have experienced a new call and have sought to respond with fidelity in service and solidarity with the poor" (p. 204).

We have already seen in the Biblical section of this essay how important the exodus paradigm is to this theology (Croatto 1981) as well as the witness of the prophetic literature and the mission of Jesus in bringing in the Reign of God with its good news to the poor (pp. 176-179).

---

[22] For the way the Bible is read in the BECs see Hennelly 1990, pp. 14-28.

What is distinctive about this theology, as relevant for our purposes in this essay, is the articulation of God's preferential option for the poor as a central theological motif. So what does this mean?

Gustavo Gutierrez points out that the term preference does not mean exclusive (Ellacuria & Sobrino 1993, p. 239). The Bible speaks of the "universality of God's love" (p. 239). Preference simply means the poor "ought to be the first" and not "the only objects of our solidarity" (p. 239). This implies a centrality. And for good reasons, since the poor are so easily overlooked.

Gutierrez goes on to point out how the poor are central to the Song of Mary (Luke 1:53), the Nazareth Manifesto (Luke 4:18-19) and are the real guests at the banquet table of the Reign of God (Matthew 22:2-10; Luke 148:14-24).

The poor both challenge the wider church to "solidarity, service, simplicity and openness to accepting the gift of God" (Hennelly 1990, p. 257) and calls the church to ongoing conversion (p. 257). Yet at the same time, commitment to the poor has brought risks, challenges and suffering and has led to martyrdom (p. 340).

While Gutierrez notes that "the option for the poor" is "one of the most important contributions to the life of the church universal" that the Liberation theologians have made (Ellacuria & Sobrino 1993, p. 250), it has not been without its problems. It has generally been passed over by the wider church (Hennelly 1990, pp. 400-401) or has been deliberately distorted to cast it in exclusive terms (p. 447).

The best way that I can describe this option for the poor is by way of a personal example. One of our children has a disability. The first priority of care was given to him without in any way not loving or neglecting our other children.

Clearly this preferential option for the poor takes the poor from the margins of history, from the periphery of society, from the heart of the slums and places them *centrally* in the very purpose of God. Evangelicals have no such theological vision.

To put all of this most simply in my own terms, but in resonance with the Liberation theologians, I would say that conversion to Christ the God of downward mobility (2 Corinthians 8:9), who becomes the poor man in history and acts on behalf of the poor, is the call for us to make a similar journey of faith, service and identification. To put that in other words: salvation invites us into personal renewal and into the purposes of God – the God of justice – and being part of the Reign of God involves having a heart for the poor.

A spirituality of liberation

The Evangelical documents of the Lausanne movement make reference to prayer (Stott 1997, pp. 44, 106, 180, 200, 218-219). The focus is on the need for intercessory prayer for evangelisation and for peace and justice to come more fully into our world (pp. 200, 219). Little attention is given to other forms of prayer and no Christian spirituality is developed in these documents, which is to animate and empower Christians in their missional activity.

With the Liberation theologians, however, who so often are regarded as being too focused on political rather than spiritual issues, there is a very significant treatment of Christian spirituality as being both at the heart of theology and in missional praxis. Very early in the development of Liberation theology as a local and missional theology emphasis was given to "a new spirituality" (Hennelly 1990, p. 185). In 1974 Claude Geffre wrote, the "mystical experience [in contemplation] presents indivisibly a double dimension of one and same original event: the meeting with the person of Christ and the experience of the presence of Christ in one's brother and sister, above all the 'least of them'" (p. 186). He also goes on to suggest that "encounter with Christ ... occurs through the mediation of the poor" (p. 186).

This double movement of prayer and contemplation is most clearly set out by the Latin American pastoral formator, Segundo Galilea. He writes that we are invited to contemplate God face to face. This involves prayer, Biblical reflection, the practice of solitude and a fruitful hearing of the voice of the Spirit. This is the movement of transcendence. But we are also invited to contemplate Christ in the face of our brothers and sisters, the neighbour, the stranger and the poor. This is the movement of incarnation. The two movements clearly belong together. This gives faith a socio-political concern and gives service a profound Christian spirituality (Galilea 1994).

This spirituality links love of God and love of neighbour (Matthew 22:37-40); the inner journey and the outer journey (Mark 1:35-39); prayer and the work of justice (Isaiah 58:6-7); and contemplation and action (Psalms 46:10; 51:10; 57:13).

Sobrino writes that in "Latin America the theology of liberation has been very attentive to spirituality" (Ellacuria & Sobrino 1993,

p. 679). This is because this spirituality is profoundly oriented both to Jesus as the *homo versu* – the true human being (p. 680) and the tragic reality people are called to live in history (p. 681). Sobrino further explains that "the authentic following of Jesus today occurs by reproducing the whole of that life in terms of the option of the poor" (p. 687). This then calls us to incarnation and the challenge of "evangelical poverty" (pp. 688-689), the holiness of love (pp. 689-690), and the need for spirit in the practice of liberation (pp. 690-693). He concludes that this spirituality is not only to empower the poor and to empower those who serve the poor, but it is also revelatory in that "the privileged place of encounter with God ... is the world of the poor" (p. 701).

Clearly these are themes that Evangelicals do not emphasise. Spirituality in the Evangelical tradition is more inward and personal. For the Liberation theologians it is inward and outward, personal and communal, spiritual and political, and makes Matthew 25 a central motif. What we have done to the least, we have done to Christ.

The church of the poor among the poor

Liberation theology did not arise in the 'sacred halls' of academia. It arose as a result of theologians and pastoral workers embedding themselves in the emerging Base Ecclesial Communities (Boff & Boff 1987, pp. 11-12). Thus this theology arose from below and as such is both an incarnational and missional theology.

The Puebla Conference, 1979, spoke of these small communities as belonging to the wider church and as being a sign of hope (Hennelly 1990, p. 249). They facilitated growth in "new interpersonal relationships in the faith, in deeper exploration of God's word, in fuller participation in the Eucharist ... and in greater commitment to justice" (p. 251).

The BECs were a new way "to *be* church and to act *as* church" (Ellacuria & Sobrino 1993, pp. 637). These are communities because they emphasise "communion and participation" (p. 638). They are ecclesial because they are linked to the "visible reality of the church" (p. 639) and they are basic because they are rooted among the poor (p. 639).

The members of the BECs study Scripture and pray and seek "to bring together what is read [in the gospels] with what is lived" (Ellacuria & Sobrino 1993, pp. 640-641). As such "there is an emphasis on the word of God, on the centrality of Jesus Christ" and an "awareness of insertion in the world ... [and the] impetus towards social transformation" (p. 641). Moreover, these communities are lay centered (p. 644). Thus it is a church from below.

Leonardo Boff (1985, 1986) has argued that the BECs are not some second rate version of church but that they are truly church. He writes there "are two expressions of the one Church of Christ." There is the institutional Church [which] supports and encourages the BECs and the BECs themselves which "are in communion with the institutional church" (Boff 1985, p. 126). Boff believes that the BECs are "a new and original way of living [the] Christian faith (p. 9) and goes on to point out how the BECs invert classical ecclesiology. The traditional Roman Catholic concept of church is God – Christ – Apostles – Bishops – Priests – Faithful. This is understood hierarchically. In the BECs we have the vision of Christ – Holy Spirit – Community – People of God – Bishop – Priest – Coordinator (p. 133).

The Lausanne documents basically assume a single monochrome form of the local church. There is no discussion of Church and para-church and missional organisations. There is no discussion of Christian community or other forms of church and there is no discussion of a church of the poor among the poor. There is an implicit assumption that the middle class church of Evangelicalism is relevant for all situations.

A missional theology

As we have already noted, Liberation theology is a local theology. Other terms such as Indigenous, ethnotheology or contextual theology are also possibilities (Schreiter 1985, pp. 5-6). What this means is that this theology has emerged in a particular context and seeks to speak to that context in the light of Scripture and the tradition of the church.

But Liberation theology is also first and foremost a missional theology (Langmead 2004, pp. 117-141). This is so because of the three mediations at the heart of this theology. The first, socio-analytical mediation, flows from an involvement with and amongst the poor in terms of missional service and discernment and analyses regarding the 'world' of poverty, injustice and oppression. The second, hermeneutical mediation, is bringing the 'world' of the poor to the Biblical text seeking God's word of life, hope and transformation. Thus the Bible is read not for its ideas or ideals, but its transformative power. The Liberation theologians are convinced that the God of justice that the Bible reveals has something to say about salvation and liberation for the poor. The third, practical mediation, is the movement praxis. Having heard from Scripture all God's people are called to the imitatio Christi and to a following of the poor Christ into the world as sign, servant and sacrament of the Reign of God (Boff & Boff 1987, pp. 24).

These three mediations, therefore, form a dynamic hermeneutic circle which moves from immersion and incarnation and being with the poor to a faithful listening to the Word of God which in turn calls us to costly and obedient service and identification. The scholar Pope-Levison (1991) in discussion of the missional theology of Segundo Galilea gives us an example of what characterises the mission theology of the Liberation theologians.

The core of evangelisation is communicating the message of salvation in Christ. To embrace salvation is to enter the Reign of God. The first epiphany of God's reign is in the person's heart. This is interior liberation. This reflects the statement of Jesus that the Kingdom of God is within you. This interior liberation means that one's values, motivations, attitudes and morals are overhauled and reoriented in and through Christ. Thus interior liberation as conversion brings about a metamorphosis in the inner person.

But this interior liberation must also move to exterior liberation. This is the epiphany of God's reign in society. This occurs when the interior liberations express themselves on the collective level, that is the formation of new relations and the transformation of society. When both occur then we have wholistic liberation. However, wholistic liberation is always promised on interior liberation because that provides the interior basis, motivation and moves to the work of transformation. In other words personal change through Christ the saviour sets *all* of God's people on the path of community, mission and service to the poor.

This integral or wholistic liberation is the overcoming of temporal servitudes and injustices (economic, social, political) through salvation in Christ. Thus Christ's salvation while deeply personal and interior, expresses itself in community, solidarity and the work of social transformation. When and where it does not, the whole notion of conversion needs to be re-thought.

This move to collective action and common participation is first of all expressed in the creation of a Christian community of brother and sisters, but this is not a closed community. It extends its boundaries through the work of wholistic liberation to the wider society and this love and care first of all needs to be extended to the little ones (the poor). This move towards the poor is premised on the community's compassion which is formed by the compassion of Christ finding its home in the inner life and the communal life of the faith community.

The work of evangelisation or wholistic liberation must be accompanied by signs or by testimony. The first sign is poverty – freedom from earthly attachments with a subsequent freedom to trust God. The notion of being poor means that the community must rely on Jesus. This means that the faith community deals with the power of Mammon through downward mobility and radical identification with the poor.

Segundo Galilea notes that Mary is an example of such evangelisation. It is an evangelisation from the periphery. It is a poor girl drawn into God's redemptive purposes whose salvation reverses the social order: the hungry are filled with good things, the rich are empty-handed (Luke 1:53).

The second sign is contemplation and contemplative prayer. In contemplation one encounters Jesus through prayer, but in contemplation one also encounters the neighbour through liberating action. Thus true contemplation encounters Jesus and our neighbours and thus integrates prayer and action. Action takes two forms – prophetic and political. Prophetic contemplative action is the proclamation of Christ's good news message of salvation, freedom and liberation. Political action seeks to alter the power structures which oppress the poor.

Unfortunately the Lausanne documents do not reflect on theological methods and discourse, but the underlying assumption is that of systematic theology and applied theology. The documents fit in the latter category. Thus unlike the Liberation theologians who locate mission at the centre of their theology with an emphasis on Trinity, Reign of God and the *missio Dei*, the Evangelical documents locate mission more in the mission of the Church. This is also the position of the Evangelical theologian Millard Erickson. The missional task is located in the discussion of the role of the church in its evangelism, edification, worship and social concern (Erickson 1995, p. 1051). This then places mission to the poor in church strategies, rather than at the very heart of who God is and God's salvific mission to the world. Mission to the poor belongs to the doctrine of God before it belongs to the mission of the church. Only in this way will service to the poor remain central. Placed only in the church's program it will remain peripheral giving the middle class captivity of the church in the Minority world and may also remain peripheral to the degree that the church in the Majority world remains captivated by the Western dream.

It seems to me that the Liberation theologians have recognised and articulated this centrality. The Lausanne documents have not.

Conclusion

In pulling together the various elements in this essay, the thematic and inter-related approach will first be reiterated, and then the challenge that the Liberation theologians have brought to Evangelicals will be restated.

The basic approach then has sought to do the following.

- In setting out a Biblical overview in relation to God's heart and our mission to the poor we have attempted to show that ministry to the poor is not peripheral to the Biblical story. It is central and at the very heart of God's love for the vulnerable and God's passion for justice and *shalom*.

- In tracing something of the history of the church's praxis in serving the poor, we note that while it fluctuated in different periods of the church's history, the commitment to serve the poor was intrinsic to the life of the church and its mission to the world.

- In setting out both the Biblical story and the service of the church in history we note that many of the themes and concerns of the Liberation theologians regarding service to the poor are not unique. However, we do believe that they have made a particular contribution regarding some key ideas and practices which we have explored in this chapter.

This then brings us to the Liberation theologians and the Evangelicals, particularly how the Liberation theologians challenge us.

- If mission is the mother of theology and all theology should be applied theology, then one of the challenges facing the Lausanne movement is to make mission a central theological construct and the documents, therefore, need to reflect a much more fully Tritarian and Reign of God theology expressing itself in the vision of *missio Dei*.

- In developing such a missional theology it is imperative, if Evangelicals wish to be closer to the Biblical story instead of to contemporary consumer and middle class values, to make God's love for the poor a more central missional motif. In other words, service to the poor is not the left-overs of our generosity. It is at the heart of God and the church's mission.

- The lack of an articulated missional spirituality amongst Evangelicals as reflected in the Lausanne documents is a sad reflection of the way in which Evangelicals have become captive to pragmatics. We are better at doing. We are poor at praying. And we have failed to place ourselves more fully in the rich Christian tradition of spirituality and the spiritual disciplines. This failure has undermined our missional response.

- At a time when there are many experiments with church, including the new emergent church movements (Frost & Hirsch 2003), new communities (Whitehead &

Whitehead 1993) and the new 'Monasticism' (The Rutba House 2005) and following the challenge of the Liberation theologians with the BECs, it is imperative that Evangelicals articulate a much more diverse and richer ecclesiology. This means that different forms of church need to emerge, including among the poor, so that the implicit normativity of the middle class is broken.

- Furthermore, I think it is high time that Evangelicals move beyond an over-focus on the personal and begin to think much more seriously about structural issues, societal evil, the nature of the powers and strategies of personal as well as social transformation.

- Finally, Evangelicals need to move beyond the hero motif regarding those who serve among the poor and make service to the poor central to become the call of all the people of God, rather than the daring few.

In conclusion

Every healthy theology and movement needs a critical component. One form is self-critique. Another form is to hear the voice of the other. That has been the strategy of this essay.

Two groups, the Liberation theologians and Evangelicals, who normally do not converse with each other, have been brought into dialogue. They have been brought together in a particular way, namely, that the former could pose a challenge to the latter. My purpose has not been to critique the Liberation theologians – though critique could also be called for. My purpose has been to challenge ourselves as Evangelicals. I hope that challenge comes home to roost, but it will be a grace if this is so. Our Australian wheat farmer is hardly likely to listen well to the Muslim rice farmer.

References

Bell, D.M. (2001). *Liberation theology after the end of history: The refusal to cease suffering*. London: Routledge.

Boerma, C. (1979). *The rich, the poor and the Bible*. Philadelphia: Westminster.

Boff, L. (1985). *Church: Charism and power*. London: SCM Press.

Boff, L. (1986). *Ecclesiogenesis: The base communities reinvent the church*. Maryknoll, NY: Orbis Books.

Boff, L., & Boff, C. (1987). *Introducing liberation theology*. Maryknoll, NY: Orbis Books.

Bosch, D.J. (1991). *Transforming mission: Paradigm shifts in theology of mission*. Maryknoll, NY: Orbis Books.

Cardenal, E. (1982). *The Gospel in Solentiname* (4 Vols). Maryknoll, NY: Orbis Books.

Costas, O.E. (1989). *Liberating news: A theology of contextual evangelism*. Grand Rapids, MI: Eerdmans.

Coutts, F. (1978). *Bread for my neighbour: The social influence of William Booth*. London: Hodder and Stoughton.

Croatto, J.S. (1981). *Exodus: A hermeneutics of freedom*. Maryknoll, NY: Orbis Books.

Ellacuria, I., & Sobrino, J. (Eds.) (1993). *Mysterium Liberationis: Fundamental concepts of liberation theology*. Maryknoll, NY: Orbis Books.

Erickson, M.J. (1995). *Christian theology.* Manila: CGM.

Evangelii Nuntiandi: Apostolic exhortation of Paul VI, on evangelisation in the modern world. (1989). Sydney: St. Paul Publications.

Ferm, D.W. (Ed.) (1986). *Third World liberation theologies: A reader.* Maryknoll, NY: Orbis Books.

Ferm, D.W. (1988). *Third World liberation theologies.* Maryknoll, NY: Orbis Books.

Flannery, A. (Ed.) (1996). *The basic sixteen documents, Vatican Council II* (Revised ed.). Northport, NY: Costello Publishing Company.

Frost, M., & Hirsch, A. (2003). *The shaping of things to come.* Peabody, MA: Hendrickson.

Galilea, S. (1994). *Following Jesus.* Quezon City, Philippines: Claretian Publications.

Gill, A. (1989). *Life on the road: The Gospel basis for a Messianic lifestyle.* Sydney: Lancer.

Gill, A. (1990). *The fringes of freedom: Following Jesus, living together, working for justice.* Sydney: Lancer.

Grenz, S.J. (2000). *Theology for the community of God.* Grand Rapids, MI: Eerdmans.

Grigg, V. (1984). *Companion to the poor.* Sydney: Albatross.

Gutierrez, G. (1983). *The power of the poor in history: Selected writings.* London: SCM Press.

Harnack, A. (1962). *The mission and expansion of Christianity in the first three centuries* [J. Moffatt, Transl. & Ed. of 1908 edition, published by Williams & Norgate, London]. New York: Harper Torchbooks.

Hempton, D. (1996). *The religion of the people: Methodism and popular religion c. 1750-1900.* London: Routledge.

Hennelly, A.T. (Ed.) (1990). *Liberation theology: A documentary history.* Maryknoll, NY: Orbis Books.

Henriot, P.J. et al. (1992). *Catholic social teaching* (Australian Edition). Melbourne: Collins Dove.

Himmelfarb, G. (1991). *Poverty and compassion: The moral imagination of the late Victorians.* New York: Vintage Books.

Hynson, L.O. (1984). *To reform the nation: Theological foundations of Wesley's ethics.* Grand Rapids, MI: Francis Asbury Press.

Kinnamon, M., & Cope, B.E. (1997). *The ecumenical movement: An anthology of key texts and voices.* Geneva: WCC Publications.

Kirk. J.A. (1985). *Liberation theology: An evangelical view from the Third World.* Basingstoke, UK: Marshall Morgan & Scott.

Laing, M. (2006). The changing face of mission: Implications for the southern shift in Christianity. *Missiology,* XXXIV(2), 165-177.

Langmead, R. (2004). *The word made flesh: Towards an incarnational missiology.* New York: University Press of America.

Lewis, D.M. (2001). *Lighten their darkness: The Evangelical mission to working-class London, 1828-1860.* New York: Greenwood Press.

Magnuson, N. (1990). *Salvation in the slums: Evangelical social work 1865-1920,* Grand Rapids, MI: Baker Book House.

McGovern, A.F. (1991). *Liberation theology and its critics: Towards an assessment.* Quezon City, Philippines: Claretian Publications.

Oliver, E.H. (1930). *The social achievements of the Christian church.* Toronto: Board of Evangelism and Social Service of the United Church of Canada.

Perkins, J. (1976). *Let justice roll down: John Perkins tells his own story.* Ventura, CA: Regal Books.

Perkins, J.M. (Ed.) (1995). *Restoring at-risk communities: Doing it together and doing it right.* Grand Rapids, MI: Baker Books.

Phan, P.C. (1984). *Social thought.* In T. Halton (Ed.), *Message of the fathers of the church.* Wilmington, DE: Michael Glazier.

Pidwell, H. (2007). *A gentle bunyip: The Athol Gill story.* West Lakes, South Australia: Seaview Press.

Pope-Levison, P. (1991) *Evangelization from a liberation perspective.* New York: Peter Lang.

Readers Digest great illustrated dictionary. (1984). 2 Vols. (Consultant Editor R. Ilson.) New York: The Readers Digest Association Ltd.

Ringe, S.H. (1985). *Jesus, liberation and the Biblical jubilee: Images for ethics and Christology.* Philadelphia: Fortress Press.

Ringma, C. (1998). *Cry freedom with voices from the Third World.* Sutherland, NSW: Albatross Books.

Ringma. C. (1999). *Gadamer's dialogical hermeneutic.* Heidelberg, Germany: Universitatsverlag C. Winter.

Ringma, C. (2003). *Seek the silences with Thomas Merton.* London: SPCK.

Ringma, C. (2004). *Let my people go with Martin Luther King, Jr.* Colorado Springs, CO: Pinon Press.

Rowland, C. (Ed.) (1999). *The Cambridge companion to liberation theology.* Cambridge, UK: Cambridge University Press.

Samuel, V., & Sugden, C. (Eds.) (1999). *Mission as transformation: A theology of the whole Gospel.* Oxford: Regnum books.

Schreiter, R.J. (1985). *Constructing local theologies.* Maryknoll, NY: Orbis Books.

Scott, W. (1980). *Bring forth justice: A contemporary perspective on mission.* Grand Rapids, MI: Eerdmans.

Segundo, J.L. (1976). *Liberation of theology.* Maryknoll, NY: Orbis Books.

Sider, R.J. (1980). *Rich Christians in an age of hunger: A Biblical study.* London: Hodder and Stoughton.

Sider, R.J. (1993). *One-sided Christianity? Uniting the church to heal a lost and broken world*. Grand Rapids, MI: Zondervan.

Sider, R.J. (1999). *Just generosity: A new vision for overcoming poverty in America*. Grand Rapids, MI: Baker Books.

Snyder, H.A. (1980). *The radical Wesley and patterns for church renewal*. Downers Grove, IL: IVP Press.

Snyder, H.A. (1991). *Models of the kingdom*. Eugene, OR: Wipf and Stock Publishers.

Stott, J. (Ed.) (1997). *Making Christ known: Historic documents from the Lausanne Movement, 1974-1989*. Grand Rapids, MI: Eerdmans.

Tamez, E. (1982). *Bible of the oppressed*. Maryknoll, NY: Orbis Books.

Taylor, W.D. (Ed.) (2000). *Global missiology for the 21st Century: The Iguassu Dialogue*. Grand Rapids, MI: Baker Academic.

The Rutba House. (Eds.) (2005). *School(s) for conversion: 12 marks of a new monasticism*. Eugene, OR: Cascade Books.

Troeltsch, E. (1960). *The social teaching of the Christian churches* (Vols I and II). New York: Harper & Row.

Washington, J.M. (Ed.) (1991). *A testament of hope: The essential writings and speeches of Martin Luther King, Jr*. New York: Harper San Francisco.

Whitehead, E.E., & Whitehead, J.D. (1993). *Community of faith: Crafting Christian communities today*. Mystic, CT: Twenty-Third Publications.

Wink, W. (1973). *The Bible in human transformation.* Philadelphia: Fortress Press.

Wright, C.J.H. (1995). *Walking in the ways of the Lord: The ethical authority of the Old Testament.* Downers Grove, IL: IVP Press.

SUPPORTING HIV PREVENTION AS PEOPLE OF FAITH

Greg Manning and Dave Andrews

Christian teaching about HIV prevention takes place in a turbulent and competitive social context. Public support for locally specific and effective HIV prevention interventions has often been slow to come from sources attributed to Christian authority or even Christian identity. In the absence of Christian consensus and collaboration for HIV prevention, unresolved conflicts among Christians, and between Christians and other population sectors have kept large Christian populations alienated and marginalised in the planning, implementation and evaluation of effective HIV prevention interventions.

In the Sermon on the Mount, Jesus addressed some problems which were not solved by traditional laws. This essay proposes that the Sermon on the Mount offers Christians a way of constructively using the conflicts related to HIV prevention to enter into new conversations with God and people, which enable reconciliation and life-giving transformation. The model we use does not offer details about the specific design for any HIV prevention intervention. HIV prevention programs, which will prevent individual infections, slow down existing epidemics and prevent new epidemics, must be designed according to the specific situation, the people involved and the information and resources available. However, the proposed model may enable Christian individuals and communities to participate in HIV prevention primarily as people of faith and faithfulness, without needing to become experts in HIV.

Conversations before regulations

In the beginning, people were expected to depend on conversations rather than regulations for guidance. The Genesis story suggests that the original idea was that people would rely on conversations with God for their sense of moral guidance, while God was "walking in the garden" (Genesis 3:8),[1] rather than on a set of legal guidelines. According to the story, people were explicitly told not to seek the knowledge of good and evil independently of their ongoing relationship with God. They were advised that to seek the knowledge of good and evil independently would lead to total disaster (as seen in Genesis 2:17).

Guidelines: Do this and you will live

When people rejected conversations with God as a means of guidance, God gave them a set of guidelines. In Exodus, God gave the people a set of regulations to help them maximise their life options and minimise the harm they did to themselves and to others. "Honour your father and your mother, so that you may live long in the land the LORD your God is giving you. You shall not murder. You shall not commit adultery. You shall not steal" and so on (Exodus 20:12-17). According to Moses, these laws were simple, accessible, practical, 'not too difficult,' do-able decrees (Deuteronomy 30:11-16) that would increase health, wealth and prosperity and minimise the harm humans

---

[1] In this essay, Scripture is taken from the Holy Bible, NEW INTERNATIONAL VERSION®. Copyright © 1973, 1978, 1984 by Biblica, Inc. All rights reserved worldwide. Used by permission.

did to each other. "Keep his commands," Moses said, "and you will live and increase" (Deuteronomy 30:16).

Harm reduction: Give them what they want

When people did not abide by God's guidelines, God still found ways to help reduce the harm their choices created. For example, God did not want men to divorce the women they married (Deuteronomy 22:19).[2] Jesus advocated for rehabilitation of a relationship through reconciliation (Matthew 5:23-24). Nonetheless, Jesus accepted Moses' legislating for divorce, acknowledging the hardness of people's hearts (Matthew 19:8). It is also clear that God never wanted the children of Israel to have their own king. After all, God was their king (Psalms 29:10; 24:8). When the people demanded a king of their own "such as all the other nations have" (1 Samuel 8:5), God tried to persuade them not to go down that track as it would reduce the people to slavery (1 Samuel 8:10-17). But the people would not listen. So God said to the prophet Samuel "listen to what they say and give them what they want" (1 Samuel 8:22). Then God directed Samuel to anoint Saul as king (1 Samuel 9:16) as the least worst option to replace God – *even though to do so was to displace God* (1 Samuel 8:7).

Jesus' Sermon on the Mount

When God came to Earth in Jesus, God offered a new range of creative ways to reduce the harmful way that the laws of Moses were being used. Some Christian scholars, like Dallas Willard, believe that the creative ways advocated by Jesus in the

---

[2] Alternative wording "a man to divorce his wife".

Sermon on the Mount were higher ideals than the lower ideals advocated by Moses (see table below). For example, Willard says Jesus calls us now to practise the *higher ideal* of 'no anger' over and above the *lower ideal* of 'no murder' (1998, p. 146ff).

The lower ideal of his society	The higher ideal of Jesus
"You have heard it was said to the people long ago, 'Do not murder, and anyone who murders will be subject to judgment'"(Matthew 5:21).	"But I tell you that anyone who is angry with his brother [or sister] will be subject to judgment. [For example] anyone who says to his brother [or sister], 'Raca,' is answerable to the Sanhedrin. And anyone who says, 'You fool!' will be in danger of the fire of hell" (Matthew 5:22)

Originally in Stassen and Gushee 2003, p. 134 and adapted by Andrews 2008, p. 46.

The trouble with this perspective is that the higher ideal advocated is a completely unrealistic ideal. In fact, the higher ideal of 'no anger' is an un-Biblical ideal. Not only is it an unrealistic ideal, none of our examples of perfection in the Bible – not even Jesus, or God – practised no anger as a principle. Not only did Jesus get angry (Matthew 21:12-17), he occasionally called opponents "fools" (Matthew 23:17).

Christian scholars, like Glen Stassen and David Gushee (2003) believe that while saintly Christian scholars like Dallas Willard are right in asserting that Jesus, in the Sermon on the Mount, was saying that his disciples needed to be able to distinguish between the initiatives he advocated and the norms his society advocated, they have been wrong in identifying those specific initiatives. They have identified as Jesus' transforming initiatives unrealistic ideals which Jesus did not advocate. Those of us who have tried to practise these unrealistic ideals as 'Gospel truth' have experienced profound disappointment.

Problems unresolved by the law

When Jesus contrasts society's *traditional norms* with his *transforming initiatives*, he doesn't simply state society's norms first and his initiatives second. First, he states society's norms. Second, he identifies the vicious cycles of unresolved problems, which society's norms do not deal with. Third, he outlines his initiatives, which can address the unresolved problems. Jesus' transforming initiatives – which are creative ways to negotiate our way through the chaos we have created – are to be found, not in his second, but in his third set of statements. This three step process in illustrated in the table below.

Traditional Norms	Vicious Cycle	Transforming Initiatives
"You have heard it was said to the people long ago, 'Do not murder, and anyone who murders will be subject to judgment'" (Matthew 5:21).	"But I tell you that anyone who is angry with his brother (or sister) will be subject to judgment. Anyone who says to his brother (or sister), 'Raca', is answerable to the Sanhedrin. And anyone who says, 'You fool!' will be in danger of the fire of hell" (Matthew 5:22).	"Therefore, if you are offering your gift at the altar and there remember that your brother (or sister) has something against you, leave your gift there in front of the altar. First go and be reconciled to your brother (or sister); then come and offer your gift. Settle matters (or make friends) quickly with your adversary who is taking you to court" (Matthew 5:23-26).
The Old Imperatives	Descriptive/Not Prescriptive	The New Imperatives

Originally from Stassen and Gushee 2003, p. 135 and adapted by Andrews 2008, p. 48.

The emphasis in the above table is not on the second point but on the third point. The imperative we are to take to heart is not an unrealistic 'no anger' policy, but a creative 'be reconciled' response to conflict resolution. Jesus advises: "Go and talk with the person, sort out the problem together, and settle the matter yourselves. At all costs, avoid going to court, because you'll both lose the shirts off your back."

Transforming initiatives

If we read the whole Sermon on the Mount from this perspective, we will note that the first sets of points indicate the old norms. Then there is a second set of points, which illustrate the mess we can make for ourselves (even if we manage to keep the old norms, and even more so if we do not!). Finally, there is a third set of points, which articulate the creative strategies Jesus suggests we can use to negotiate our way through the mess that we are in. The transforming initiatives that Jesus advocates we use to reduce the harm we do are all spirited personal and relational processes which take us beyond the law as we know it. They describe a return to modest relationship with God and other people – a return to the conversations we began with in Genesis.

Traditional Norms	Vicious Cycle	Transforming Initiatives
1. Do not kill.	Being so angry that you are abusive, can be brutal too.	Go, be reconciled.
2. Do not commit adultery.	But a slow-burn lust is adultery in your heart.	So remove yourself from the temptation (Mark 9:43-50).

3. You can divorce.	But divorce usually involves infidelity.	Be reconciled (1 Corinthians :7-11).
4. Do not swear falsely.	But taking any oath suggests making false claims.	Let your 'Yes' be 'Yes' and your 'No' be 'No'.
5. Take an eye for an eye, and a tooth for a tooth.	But retaliating entails returning evil for evil.	Turn the other cheek, give what you are asked for.
6. Love your neighbour and hate your enemy.	But hating enemies does not deal with enmity.	Love your enemies, bless those who curse you.
7. Contributing publicly ...	... is parading your charity not practising generosity.	Give without advertising it.
8. Fasting publicly ...	... is parading your piety not practising sincerity.	Fast without publicising it.
9. Praying publicly ...	... is parading your religiosity, not practising spirituality.	Pray authentically in secret.
10. Lots of prayer ...	... is simply repeating a lot of empty sacred phrases.	Make the Lord's Prayer the prayer of your heart.
11. Pile up treasures on earth (Luke 12:16-31).	But thieves break in and steal.	Store up treasures in heaven.
12. No one can serve two different masters.	It is impossible to serve God and money at the same time.	Store up treasures in heaven.
13. Do not judge lest you be judged.	If you judge you will be judged by the very same standards.	So take the plank out of your own eye before you take the speck out of your neighbour's eye.
14. Do not throw your pearls before swine.	They will trample on them and then tear you to pieces.	The only one you can totally entrust yourself to – is God!

Originally from Stassen and Gushee 2003, p. 142 and adapted by Andrews 2008, pp. 50-51.

Destroying *the dividing wall of hostility*: Creating a hospitable space for a conversation

In the Sermon on the Mount, Jesus said, "Do not think I have come to abolish the Law or the Prophets; I have come not to abolish them but to fulfill them" (Matthew 5:17). So it is clear that Jesus was not interested in abolishing a single letter in the law prohibiting killing, stealing and lying; Jesus wanted to embody a divine nonviolent ethos that fulfilled the spirit of the law and fleshed it out in positive, proactive, practical actions.

However, according to the Apostle Paul, when "the law with all its commandments and regulations" became a "barrier" that was "the dividing wall of hostility" between people who defined themselves over against others by their identification with the law – their relationship to the law, their access to the law, their interaction with the law, their interpretation of the law, their submission to the law and their defence of the law – Jesus had no hesitation in abolishing "the law with all its commandments and regulations" (Ephesians 2:14).

We might paraphrase Paul's letter to the Ephesians by saying:

> Remember some of you were called 'victims of HIV/AIDS' by those who had made sure they weren't caught dead with the virus. As such you were excluded from church, not included in their community, and "without hope – even in God – in their world." But the good news is that when God came in Christ, he destroyed the barrier, the big brick wall, "the dividing wall of hostility" that existed between you and everyone else, by delegitimising the moral, legal and religious

arguments based on the Bible (that so-called 'people of God' had used to justify their prejudice against you) through his undeniable unconditional love for you. So you are no longer to be treated as victims of discrimination, but as brothers and sisters in God's family. Let the family conference begin (Ephesians 2:11-21).

Guidelines for HIV prevention

Two traditional norms, which have been applied by Christians as HIV prevention strategies are *Abstain from sex outside of marriage*, and *Be faithful to your spouse* (who is assumed to be HIV negative). These two guidelines have popularly received approval by Christian authorities for preventing new HIV infections. Since well before the discovery of AIDS, abstinence from sex outside marriage and fidelity to a spouse reflect Christian longing to be faithful to the teachings of the Bible and to be pure and holy people who please God. The longing to be 'holy people who please God' remains intact for Christians who are committing themselves to slow down the spread of HIV (e.g. World Evangelical Alliance's resolution, *HIV – A Call to Action*, 2008).

There are many problem statements, challenging the adequacy and effectiveness of preaching abstinence and fidelity as HIV prevention. For the purpose of accelerating the participation of Christian communities in coordinated and effective HIV prevention efforts, we have chosen only three problems. These problems define specific barriers contributing to the marginalisation of Christians in HIV prevention.

1. *Abstinence and fidelity are not the only ways of*

preventing HIV infection. Developments in science and technology have provided useful tools which have enabled the prevention of HIV infections and epidemics.

2. *Associating HIV prevention with Christian holiness and purity fuels stigma* by incorrectly linking HIV infection to individuals' sin or belief.

3. *Abstinence and fidelity are preached as the choices that individuals make.* HIV infection requires more than legally, culturally and economically constructed situations, which often prevent individuals from using their knowledge to protect their health.

1 Science and technology

Advances in science and technology have enabled many individuals and populations to prevent new HIV infections and epidemics, as well as slow down existing epidemics, despite widespread sexual activity outside of marriage. Laboratory tests have enabled blood banks and blood products to be kept free from HIV. They have also enabled individuals and governments to assess and monitor their own specific HIV prevention needs. Medical treatment and infant feeding options may help pregnant women to prevent HIV infection associated with childbirth. Medical treatment also reduces the likelihood that HIV will be transmitted by sexually active people who are living with HIV. Disposable injecting equipment, and sterilization procedures have protected injecting drug users, as well as people receiving medical injections, from HIV infection. The latex barriers provided by male and female condoms have also effectively prevented the sexual transmission of HIV in individual relationships, and within sexually active populations. Preventing sexual intercourse itself (i.e. abstinence), and preventing sexual intercourse with an infected person (e.g. faithfulness to an uninfected spouse) define contexts in which HIV cannot spread. In addition to these 'primary' prevention strategies, the informed use of science and technology makes preventing the transmission of HIV possible in situations where there is a chance of HIV transmission. It has enabled people and populations to prevent HIV infections where there is sexual activity in the presence of HIV, where there is drug use in the presence of HIV, where there is reproduction in the presence of HIV and where blood and blood products are required even after HIV has been identified in the local population.

To date, there is neither a popular, nor authoritative Christian consensus about the role and use of technology in HIV prevention. Supporting condom promotion and needle exchange programs has been prominently controversial in Christian discourse around HIV prevention. However, the ongoing debates related to technology go beyond condoms and needles, to include testing, medication and research. While there is not a consensus about the role and use of technology, there is a growing consensus that Christians must be constructively involved in HIV prevention efforts at personal, local, national and international levels.

Most HIV prevention programs are nationally coordinated programs, which regularly evaluate their effectiveness in preventing new infections and slowing down the spread of HIV. Therefore, Christians who want to participate in the planning and monitoring of HIV prevention programs must be able to interact with people who advocate the effective and life-saving role of technology in HIV prevention programming. The content of these conversations will include specific information about specific epidemics under discussion, numerical targets showing how various HIV prevention strategies might affect the epidemic, and ways of monitoring HIV prevention efforts so that prevention efforts can respond to the specific requirements of the epidemics under consideration.[3] Even with all of the scientific research about HIV, the epidemics and ways of preventing the spread of HIV, the design of HIV prevention programs is based on passionate conversations between different groups of people.

2 Stigma

Traditionally, Christians have described divergence from 'abstinence' and 'fidelity' using words such as 'fornication,' 'adultery' and 'infidelity'. These five powerful and evocative words are names used for describing specific virtues and sins, which are defined in relation to the moral and legal code of marriage. In the context of HIV prevention, they are highly stigmatising words, which nurture the inaccurate and misleading assumption that HIV infection is an indicator of an individual's sexual immorality. This assumption creates stigma which is fuelled by the religious language of righteousness and unrighteousness.

Stigma aids the spread of HIV and accelerates the death of people who are living with HIV by undermining the healthy and supportive options that may be available to people in crisis. People may not want to know their HIV status, or may not want to seek care and support even if they know they are HIV

---

[3] More information about the principles, policies, programs and strategies can be found in UNAIDS (2005) *Intensifying HIV prevention: UNAIDS policy position paper*, Joint United Nations Programme on HIV/AIDS and UNAIDS (2007) *Practical guidelines for intensifying HIV prevention: Towards universal access*, UNAIDS.

positive, for fear of judgement and social exclusion.

Financial spending by the US on HIV prevention in Africa is the largest financial investment in HIV prevention in the world. It is called the President's Emergency Plan for AIDS Relief (PEPFAR). This spending has significantly influenced international Christian thought and discussion about HIV prevention in the first decade of the 21st century. It has maintained the focus of Christian understandings and discussion about HIV prevention on preaching and enabling abstinence and fidelity. While encouraging Christians to continue to preach abstinence and fidelity, PEPFAR itself has taken two important steps away from the stigmatising language of righteousness and unrighteousness.

Firstly, PEPFAR monitors the effects of the preaching of abstinence before marriage and fidelity within marriage without reference to the moral and legal framework of marriage. In order to do this, PEPFAR monitors the *age of sexual debut* of individuals and the *number of an individual's sex partners* within a specified time period. The removal of the reference to the moral and legal code for the purposes of monitoring and evaluation is not an abandonment of morality and law. The call to abstinence and fidelity (within marriage) is still intact. However, the stigmatising language of judgement has been removed so that people can talk about how they are responding to the preaching without fear of judgement. This transforming initiative represents a movement towards a language of grace and security which is part of overcoming stigma. In effect, it enables the honest conversations about sexual behaviour and experience, which are essential for the design, implementation, monitoring and evaluation of HIV prevention initiatives.

Secondly, PEPFAR evaluates the effectiveness of the preaching of abstinence and fidelity in terms of the increase in the average age of sexual debut and the decrease in the average number of sexual partners *across a population*. Populations include people for whom the preaching of abstinence and fidelity has been effective HIV prevention, as well as people who do not practise abstinence and fidelity, as well as people who remain vulnerable to HIV infection and who are living with HIV, despite their own abstinence and/or fidelity.

The acknowledgement of entire populations is another critical transformation that the traditional preaching of abstinence and fidelity must undergo to have a meaningful role in HIV prevention. HIV prevention planning involves interacting with sectors of the population who remain vulnerable to HIV infection, regardless of how effective HIV prevention has been to date. In some places, this means the conversations must involve drug users, sex workers, prisoners and men who have sex with other men. In other places, this conversation will also include young people, married women, or migrant labourers.

Despite attempts to reduce stigma associated with focusing on abstinence and fidelity as HIV prevention strategies, these strategies are still considered to be stigmatising by many. The African Network of religious leaders living with or personally affected by HIV and AIDS (ANERELA+) argues that the ABC[4] model for prevention reinforces the stigmatisation of people who are living with HIV by suggesting that people who are living with HIV were immoral (i.e. either not abstinent outside of marriage or unfaithful to their spouse) and

---

[4] ABC stands for 'Abstain from sexual activity', 'Be faithful to your sexual partner', and 'consistently and correctly use condoms.'

unwilling to protect themselves from infection (World Wide Council of Churches 2006). ANERELA+ promotes an alternative model called SAVE, which stands for Safe practices, Access to treatments, Voluntary counseling and testing, and Empowerment (of children, youth, men, women, communities and nations).

The SAVE model includes space for conversations with people who may want to talk about the role of technology in preventing HIV transmission. It also asserts a need to relate to people who are already living with HIV in HIV prevention, by locating medical treatment within the prevention framework. People who are living with HIV are claiming an unmarginalised role in preventing the transmission of HIV, with campaign slogans such as 'Positive Prevention' and 'HIV stops with me/us'.

3 Justice

Christian preaching and monitoring of abstinence and fidelity focuses on individuals, and specifically Christian individuals. The widespread infection of married women in Africa, who have chosen abstinence before marriage and fidelity to their spouse, has dramatically exposed the inadequacy of preaching HIV prevention messages to individuals alone.

Gender inequality is a major driver of HIV epidemics. The ABC strategy does not help females to protect themselves from HIV infection, because in many places, they have little control over when they have sex (i.e. they cannot choose to abstain), over whom their male partner has sex with (i.e. they cannot control their partner's fidelity), and whether their male partner uses a condom consistently, or even at any time at all (Phiri 2007).

Many women are not able to make choices about their sexual behaviour. The sexual experience of many women is controlled by husbands and other men, family members, and cultural and legal factors. In such settings, the choices by women for abstinence and fidelity often do not protect them from vulnerability to sexually transmitted HIV infection. The gender-oriented analysis calls for the transformative initiative of a commitment to gender justice, including the redemptive transformation of patriarchal structures, cultural practices and dangerous masculinities (including violence and silence about gender-based violence, inequality and injustice) along with the empowerment of women.

Conclusion: Transformations and a return to conversations

Preventing new HIV infections, new HIV epidemics and slowing down existing epidemics are urgent and ongoing tasks. Many Christians believe that the Gospel, and faith guided by the Biblical texts, is capable of informing and supporting effective HIV prevention strategies at the beginning of the 21st century. However, many urgent Christian statements about HIV prevention have advocated a high ideal for all, regardless of such issues as belief, gender, and socio-economic situation. Many have chosen to defend traditional Christian teaching about sex in relation to marriage as HIV prevention, without recognising or acknowledging the complexities of HIV infection and HIV epidemics.

The marginalisation of Christians in HIV prevention efforts is a natural outcome of advocating a 'higher ideal'. Firstly, the high ideal leaves no room for specific problems, specific situations and specific epidemics. Secondly, it is difficult to talk about a complex and urgent problem that has no universal solution, such as the spread of HIV, with a partner who wants to talk only in ideals about how things 'should' be.

The model we are proposing enables more rapid entry for Christians into HIV prevention initiatives, which are still urgently required. The participation is considered more rapid because people and communities can enter as people of faith, without first needing to become experts in HIV.

The principles of this model are:

- acknowledge sacred traditions and identity,
- be ready to learn and face conflict and challenge in a spirit of reconciliation, and
- work with other people, and different groups in creative, life-giving conversations and actions.

In the Sermon on the Mount, Jesus uses three steps to critique the effectiveness of traditional and sacred laws intended to help communities to live long, safe, responsible and prosperous lives.

The first step is a **recognition and affirmation of** *traditional guidelines.* This step involves a humble assertion of one's identity and what is important within that identity (e.g. sexual purity, marital fidelity, specific laws, feeding one's children). Besides religious laws, traditional guidelines may include cultural or economic practices, as well as popular strategies which have already emerged in response to various HIV epidemics. This first step allows entire populations to participate in HIV prevention by coming as themselves and bringing what is important to them into the discussion.

The second step is to **clearly state the problems that arise** from using the traditional guidelines for HIV prevention. The problem statement must be relevant and accurate in order to support effective prevention initiatives. Besides there being many problems to address, there are also many competing problem statements. The definition of the problem can itself be a source of great conflict. The definition of problems will be more accurate if people who are directly affected by a problem which is not resolved by the traditional norms are involved in the definition of the problem.

The third step is to **enable life-saving action** which can achieve what the traditional norm was not able to achieve. Just as it requires many different perspectives to define a problem accurately, there will be many different roles required to create a situation in which the response can be effectively attempted. Some of these actions will be direct, while others will be supportive or indirect.

Jesus' process in the Sermon on the Mount does not conclude with an eternal absolute law. It is a cycle, which enables the life-saving actions to be critiqued whenever they become like traditional norms. In his own response to two problematic male orientations (i.e. lustful gazing upon women and divorce), Jesus suggested two hyperbolic solutions (i.e. "pluck out your eye" and "cut off your hand") that from time to time have been interpreted literally as violent instructions – which have set up their own vicious cycles of unresolved problems that have needed to be critiqued as traditional norms in pursuit of further life-saving actions.

This model also recognises that HIV prevention programs change over time. Prevention strategies are affected by new information and changing resources. Prevention strategies change as epidemics change. 'Successful' interventions among certain populations will cause the attention of HIV prevention to shift. For example, in Cambodia, slowing down the spread of HIV among men who were infected when they visited sex workers, highlighted that there were many women who were married to the infected men, who were not supported by HIV prevention efforts. On the other hand, when the spread of HIV is not controlled in specific (and often stigmatised) populations, such as injecting drug users, it can spread to more generalised populations, and HIV prevention efforts are required to protect unstigmatised families. The traditional norms of HIV prevention must always be evaluated to test their effectiveness. In 2008, The Joint United Nations Programme on HIV/AIDS (UNAIDS) "called on countries to realign their prevention programmes by better understanding how the most recent infections were transmitted and the reasons why they occurred," saying, "Not only will this approach help prevent the next 1,000 infections in each community, but it will also make money for AIDS work more effectively and help put forward a long-term and sustainable AIDS response."[5] According to the model we are proposing, people from the populations most affected (e.g. where the most recent infections occurred) must be part of the conversation to define the problems which are not resolved by the prevailing norms.

---

[5] www.un.org/apps/news/story.asp?NewsID=29121&Cr=HIV&Cr1=UNAIDS accessed 6 June 2010.

Jesus' method in the Sermon on the Mount is a return to the conversations between men, women and God. Conversations are important in both the description of the problem arising from the current norms, as well as in formulating creative responses to the problem. The table below summarises the description of three problems which are unresolved by preaching abstinence and fidelity as HIV prevention, as well as some associated transforming initiatives. It also indicates something about the conversations which are necessary in the process, including who might be involved in those conversations, and the likely content of those conversations.

Description of unresolved problem of vicious cycle	Transforming initiative	Conversations
Abstinence and fidelity are not the only ways of preventing HIV infection.	Understand and use the science and technology available for HIV prevention.	*People who advocate various uses of science and technology.* These discussions will require scientific information about the specific epidemics and prevention strategies under discussion, as well as measurable prevention targets and ways of monitoring and evaluating prevention efforts.
Associating HIV prevention with Christian holiness and purity fuels stigma by inappropriately linking HIV infection to sin or belief.	Remove judgmental language. Focus on entire populations more than individuals.	*People who are living with HIV* are essential in the design of prevention models. *People who are most vulnerable to infection* must be involved as leaders in discussions about HIV prevention.

Description of unresolved problem of vicious cycle	Transforming initiative	Conversations
Decisions about abstinence, the fidelity of their 'mate,' and consistent male condom use, and access to testing and treatment are not decisions that females can make, whether or not they are married.	Gender justice, including the redemptive transformation of patriarchal structures, cultural practices and dangerous masculinities (including violence and silence about gender-based violence, inequality and injustice) along with the empowerment of women.	*Men and women* in their local cultures and within church structures (including marriage and family).

If we are to follow the example of Jesus in our engagement with HIV prevention, we need to move beyond simply re-stating our commitment to religious norms, and begin to discuss the limitations of those existing norms. We have to start to talk about experimenting with possible life-saving initiatives that might effectively solve the problems that simple adherence to the existing norms cannot solve. And – in order to do this properly – we will need to have open, ongoing conversations with stigmatised people, just like Jesus did.

References

Andrews D. (2008). *Plan be: Be the change you want to see in the world.* Milton Keynes, UK: Authentic.

Phiri, I. A. (2007). Gender, religion and HIV and AIDS prevention. In M.W. Dube (Ed.), *Theology in the HIV and AIDS Era Series.* Produced by Ecumenical HIV and AIDS Initiative in Africa.

Stassen, G., & Gushee, D. (2003). *Kingdom ethics.* Downers Grove, IL: IVP Press.

UNAIDS (2005). *Intensifying HIV prevention: UNAIDS policy position paper.* Joint United Nations Programme on HIV/AIDS.

UNAIDS (2007). *Practical guidelines for intensifying HIV prevention: Towards universal access.* UNAIDS.

Willard, D. (1998). *The divine conspiracy.* San Francisco: Harper.

World Council of Churches. (2006). *Towards a policy on HIV/AIDS in the workplace: A working document.* Final Version 20 January 2006. Geneva: WCC.

World Evangelical Alliance (2008). *HIV – A call to action.*

AUSTRALIA - WHOSE LAND? A CHRISTIAN CALL FOR RECOMPENSE[1]

Dr Peter Adam

Introduction

This is an important issue, one of the great issues facing Australia. I am not an expert and do not have first-hand experience of the human suffering that lies within the question. So I am in danger of being glib in the face of an immense tragedy which has engulfed Australia since 1788, and in the face of the ongoing effects of that tragedy still present all around us.

However, I am saying what needs to be said, and I want to encourage Christians to take leadership in these matters.

I ask forgiveness from those Indigenous readers for whom these matters are immeasurably and constantly painful. I assure you of my deep respect for you and for your full human dignity as men and women made in the image of God. I want to honour you and your people. I hope that nothing I write will offend

---

[1] This essay is the adapted transcript of a lecture first given in August 2009 at Morling College Sydney, as the second Annual John Saunders Lecture. The John Saunders Lecture is sponsored by the Baptist Union of NSW Social Issues Committee and seeks to address contemporary social and ethical issues in Australia from a scholarly evangelical perspective.
The Revd John Saunders (1806-1859) was an evangelical Christian with a missionary heart, a keen intellect, a gift for public speaking, and a passion for Christian social responsibility. He is best known for his temperance work and his advocacy for justice for the Aborigines. His famous sermon on Aboriginal justice has been anthologised in several places, most recently in Sally Warhaft (Ed.) (2004). *Well May We Say ... The Speeches That Made Australia*. Melbourne: Black Inc.
The lecture has also been given at Malyon College Brisbane and at Ridley College Melbourne.

you or hurt you. I want this essay to express the duty and debt of love that I owe you.

Our question is, 'Australia – whose land?'

1. Australia is God's land, given to the Indigenous peoples of this land.

In his book *The Discarded Image*, C. S. Lewis points to the immense contrast between the ways in which a person in Medieval Europe thought about the universe, and the ways modern people of the West think about the universe. He pictures a Medieval person going out to look at the stars on a cloudless night. Though that person would have thought that the earth was the geographical centre of the universe, looking at the stars he or she would have felt as if they were looking into the centre of reality, to God's heaven, looking from the outside into the centre. A modern Western person knows that the earth is not the centre of the universe, yet, when looking 'up' at the stars, feels that the earth is the centre and that the stars are 'out there' (1964, p. 199).

Similarly, modern Western people assume that what they use belongs to them, that they own the land. They dislike a God who intrudes into their space, and makes claims on their possessions. For modern Westerners have lost the idea that land and universe belongs, not to ourselves, but to another, to God.

Yet God created all lands, all peoples, all that is; and God sustains all lands, all peoples, and all that is. The air we breathe, the water we drink, the food we eat, the bodies and minds and hearts that we are, all these are God's constant gifts. If God did not sustain the universe, it would not exist. Not a sparrow falls to the ground without God our Father knowing and caring (Matthew 10:29)[2] and, as all animals receive their daily food from God (Psalm 104:27), so do we all, whether we know it or not. God created this land, its rugged natural beauty, its diverse and unusual flora and fauna, its mountains, deserts, its rivers and seas.

And God, who created all lands, distributed lands to the peoples of the world. For, as Paul preached at Athens, "God ... made from one ancestor all nations to inhabit the whole earth, and allotted the times of their existence, and boundaries of the places where they would live" (Acts 17:26).

So all lands belong to God, and he distributed them to many nations, setting the time and places where they would live. The land is God's land. To respect and honour God was to know that he made Australia, and to treat the Indigenous peoples who were here in 1788 with respect. The appalling theory of *terra nullius* treated people as if they had no significance. This was an insult to them, and an offence against God their maker.

Sometimes God re-allocates land, as recounted in Deuteronomy 2:20-22 when he dispossessed the Rephaim or Zamzummin to make room for the Ammonites, and dispossessed the Horim, to make room for the Edomites. More famously, God dispossessed the nations of the land of Caanan, to make room for his people, the Israelites. But this does not mean that every dispossession of land is the will of God. The normal situation is

---

[2] Scripture references are taken from the New Revised Standard Version Bible, copyright 1989, Division of Christian Education of the National Council of the Churches of Christ in the United States of America. Used by permission. All rights reserved.

expressed in Amos 1 and 2, where Damascus, Gaza, Tyre, Edom, Ammon and Moab are condemned because of their attacks on their neighbouring peoples. So there we read that the Ammonites ripped open pregnant women in Gilead in the process of enlarging their territory (Amos 2:13-15), and for those sins, God sent them into exile. Even nations used by God to judge his own people, were condemned for unnecessary violence in that judgement (Zechariah 1:15). And great Babylon is condemned because "in her was found the blood ... of all who have been slain on earth" (Revelation 18:24).

In many situations we do not know if God's will includes the re-allocation of land. However, our best moral rule for individuals and nations is to assume that theft is wrong. Even if we suspected that someone did not have full legal rights to the land on which they lived, we would not think it right to dispossess them: why would our rights be any more legitimate?

God in his mercy may have worked some things for good when the Europeans arrived in Australia, despite much that was evil. But that does not make that act of conquest an act of the will of God. Europeans assume that theft is wrong, and our legal codes support that view. We do not assume that every theft reflects the will of God. Why should we think that the theft of land is any different?

Some European invaders of North America may have thought that they were God's chosen people, as they dispossessed the Indigenous people as the people of Israel dispossessed the Canaanites. But it was a bold and unsustainable claim, and resulted in a mortal sin. Our actions in Australia may not have been based on that false Biblical claim, but were in effect sins as serious as those Americans. Pitched battles by Government troops at Richmond in 1795, at Parramatta in 1797, at Bathurst in 1824 or Pinjarra in 1834 (Harris 1998, p. 432) were as appalling as local murders by thugs and thieves. It was, as Laurence Threkeld of the London Missionary Society wrote in 1837, "a war of extermination" (in Harris 1998, p. 432). Of course there is a danger of overstating ownership of land and reverence for it. We European Australians are not free of the guilt of a kind of secular idolatry of the land. Even the people of Israel learnt that they could serve God in exile, and that in long term Salvation History, the land pointed beyond itself to a great and more substantial reality, a "better country," "the city whose builder and maker is God" (Hebrews 11:10,16). But loving our neighbours includes respecting their property. Here is a reasonable question: "How could this white man come onto our land and start pushing us around?" (in Seiffert 2008, p. 29).

But, are there not many examples of invasion and the taking over ownership of land?

Yes, there have been many examples in human history of invasion and the taking over of the ownership of land. Similarly, there have been many examples of private theft over the history of the human race. We would not therefore defend or justify theft. It is one of the weaknesses of evangelical Christians that we are very aware of the rights of individuals, but less aware of the rights of groups of people or of nations. If someone stole our property, we would try to recover it. Similarly if the Japanese had successfully invaded Australia and taken possession of it, we would have fought to regain possession of it.

Surely the principle of original gift is now unworkable?

In some cases, it is impossible to know the nation to whom God first gave some land, and they may not exist at the present time. That is not the case in Australia. We know those to whom God gave the land, and we know when it was stolen from them. It is time for sorrow, repentance, and reparation for the European invasion and capture of Australia, similar to when the Council of Berlin in 1884 carved up Africa between Germany, France, England, Belgium, Italy, and Portugal. Australia is a particularly clear example of the continuity of Indigenous ownership and possession of the land. The curious and painful fact is that while England and the other European nations have returned the African land to Indigenous ownership, that has not happened in Australia, New Zealand, the United States of America, or Canada. The British left India and the British, Germans, French Belgians and Portuguese left Africa and the Dutch left Indonesia, why has it not happened here? Perhaps we still need more winds of change. The practical answer is that the Indigenous Indians, Africans and Indonesians were clearly in the majority, whereas in Australia, New Zealand, Canada and the United States of America they were not. However, that is to say that genocide is to be rewarded. It would in fact be possible, even if very difficult and complicated for Europeans and others to leave Australia. I am not sure where we would go, but that would be our problem.

Ahab was an ungodly king of Samaria (1 Kings 21). He wanted the vineyard of Naboth, which was Naboth's ancestral inheritance, given to his family by God. Jezebel, Ahab's wife, caused Naboth's murder, so that Ahab could take the vineyard. God sent the prophet Elijah with these two accusations: "Have you killed, and also taken possession?" (1 Kings 21:19). How would those European settlers have answered those questions?

We have already thought about Paul's words in Acts 17:26: "God, who made from one ancestor all nations to inhabit the whole earth, and allotted the times of their existence, and boundaries of the places where they would live." We have committed a great crime. We have failed to acknowledge that God allotted nations times and boundaries in this land. In order to commit these sins, we have committed the even greater sin of failing to acknowledge that we all come from one ancestor, that we are *one blood*, that we are brothers and sisters of the Indigenous peoples of this land. The doctrine of *terra nullius* treated people as if their existence had no meaning. But we must not treat people that way. For, as Calvin preached, the duty to love our neighbour extends to all.

> Since [God] has stamped his image upon us, and since we share a common nature, this ought to inspire us to provide for one another. The one who seeks to be exempt from the care of his neighbour is disfiguring himself and declaring that he no longer wishes to be a man. For whilst we are human beings, we must see our own faces reflected, as by a mirror, in the faces of the poor and despised, who can go no further and who are trembling under their burdens, even if they are people who are most alien to us. If a Moor or a barbarian comes to us, because he is a man, he is a mirror in which we see reflected the fact that he is our brother and our neighbour; for we cannot change the rule of nature that God has established as immutable (1997, pp. 624-625).[3]

God's commandments are clear: "You shall not murder ...

---

[3] Calvin's sermon on Galatians 6:9-11.

you shall not steal ... you shall not covet" (Exodus 20:13-17). But we Europeans coveted space for a penal colony, new land, new opportunities, and great wealth. We coveted, and so we stole, and we stole, and so we murdered. We read in the Law: "Cursed be anyone who moves a neighbour's boundary marker" (Leviticus 27:17). We not only moved the boundary markers, we removed them, and stole the land.

As one Christian commented in 1923 (*Neighbours of the Never-Never*), in language of the time:

> The white men ... took the best of the land for their sheep and cattle, killing the black men's food ... The blacks tried to drive these settlers out of their country ... but the white men were not to be driven back. They armed themselves and made open war upon these poor blacks ... As we look back over these years there is much that we have to be ashamed of (cited in Harris 1998, p. 449).

We can see the simple error of the Christians of Connecticut who expressed their views in these words in 1640: "Voted, that the earth is the Lord's and the fullness thereof; voted, that the earth is given to the Saints; voted, that we are the Saints" (Willison 1964, p. 421).

However we have condoned the same action without any theological justification. A pioneer worker with Indigenous people, John Gribble, said:

> If I am to work as a missionary, it must be on the lines of justice and right to the Aborigines of this land, in opposition to the injustice and wrong-doing of unprincipled white men. This is my decision and by it I

stand or fall. (Harris, 'John Gribble' cited in Dickey 1994, pp. 137-138).

2. It is right to apologise.

It is right to say, 'Sorry'. For they were serious crimes and sins. They included the theft of land, which was not only the theft of livelihood, but also the theft of home, identity, and religion. They included murder and manslaughter, the destruction of social structures and culture, the breaking up of families, the desecration of the dead, and genocide, with no legitimate justification.

But are we responsible for the sins of others?

My ancestors arrived from England, Scotland, Ireland and Wales in the 1850s. As far as I know, none of them killed any Indigenous people. But we have benefited from death and dispossession, and have grown wealthy from the poverty of others. If I discovered that my grandfather had killed a man, impoverished his family, and plundered his property to enrich himself, I think that I would try to find any descendants of the murdered man, and at least say sorry. For I would have benefited from that crime.

But what of the defence that many Europeans did not intend to do evil?

No doubt there were some who did not intend to do evil, who did not realise the evil that they did, who intended to do good but who did evil, or who intended to keep at a distance, and so were complicit in the evil deeds of others. We have to face the fact that unintended evil still has grave consequences. If, by accident, I killed a person while driving my car, I still have to face the reality of what has happened. In that situation, whatever the legal judgement, I would still think it right to go to the family of the person whom I had killed to say sorry.

Do churches have any responsibilities in these matters?

Why yes, because the land and wealth of churches came from land that had been stolen from the Indigenous people of Australia. I was Vicar of St Jude's Anglican Church in Carlton, Victoria. The land on which the church was build was a *Crown Grant*. That meant that the government stole the land and gave it to the church. We received stolen goods. However, even if we had bought the land from another owner or from the government, it would still have originally been stolen land. The prosperity of our churches has come from the proceeds of crime. Saying sorry is the least we should do. So our houses, our churches, our colleges, our shops, our sports grounds, our parks, our courts, our parliaments, our prisons, our hospitals, our roads, our reservoirs are stolen property. Churches that know the Scriptures and so know the will of God should be the first to say sorry.

3. It is time to repent.

However saying sorry is not enough. We need to repent.

Saying sorry may just mean remorse, feeling sorry for ourselves, more self-pity.

Saying sorry may mean no more than regretting that others

feel they have been badly treated, without acknowledging that anything wrong has happened.

Saying sorry might just mean that we recognise that bad things have happened, without acknowledging that we have committed sin for which we are objectively guilty.

Saying sorry for the harm we have done to others, does not necessarily mean that we also acknowledge that any sin against another person is also a sin against God and before God, and for which we face God's judgement.

Saying sorry does not necessarily entail a decision that we will not continue in the sin, or continue to benefit from it, or that we intend to remedy the wrong we have done.

It is time to repent, to turn from our sin, to acknowledge our sin before God. Repentance must lead to recompense, as we will see. Christian believers around Australia would be horrified at the thought of murdering their neighbours in order to steal their property, and would be highly offended if we suggested that they might do such things. But we have benefited because others have done these actions for us and we continue to live off the proceeds of those crimes and sins.

Our guilt is great. If we are tempted to excuse ourselves by thinking that perhaps God was punishing the Indigenous people of the land by sending the Europeans, then we must acknowledge that we have committed greater sins. We prided ourselves on our civilisation and our Christianity. We have greater responsibility, and greater guilt, and should prepare ourselves to be invaded and cast out of the land when the time is right.

For nations' sin, as John Saunders reminds us in a sermon he preached in 1838:

> It is not for us to state in what degree this principle shall be applied to any particular people, nor to predict the precise moment of its application, but we may be sure that the unchanging word of God has been fulfilled, and is still accomplished toward every one of the tribes of Adam. The measure of forbearance, the weight of visitation, and the time of indignation are in the hands of the Eternal, but the certainty of a righteous retribution towards all is clearly established.
>
> An additional point is also obvious, that if there be anything which falls for a swifter and a more severe punishment than another, it is the shedding of human blood. For this the nations receive a prompt and condign visitation. Oppression, cruelty and blood, gather the clouds of vengeance, and provoke the threatening thunder of the Omnipotent, and attract the bolt of wrath. "Who so sheddeth man's blood by man shall his blood be shed," was the decree of the Eternal when the life of the brutes was placed in human power, and the reason for this solemn distinction is "for in the image of God made he man." And this is a distinction which God has maintained, does maintain, and will maintain till the end of time.
>
> It is a fearful thing to shed human blood, it is an act which has the deepest malefaction of heaven upon it –

a curse from the dread power above ... Pilate might wash his hands but he could not make himself guiltless of innocent blood.

We may feel that God is only concerned with the sins of individuals, that there are no shared sins. However, the Bible is deeply concerned with the sins of communities, from the sins of the people of God in the Old Testament to the sins of the church at Corinth, as when Paul calls on the church to be reconciled to God.

We may think that we are not the ones to repent, because we did not commit the sins. However, although the Bible teaches that we may not blame the sins of our ancestors for our suffering in order to claim that we are innocent (Ezekiel), it also give examples of repentance for the sins of ancestors. One is found in Daniel's prayer, when he confessed "my sin and the sin of my people Israel" (Daniel 9:20). Daniel confessed the sins of his community and of his ancestors, corporate and ancestral sin.

> I prayed to the LORD my God and made confession, saying, "Ah, Lord, great and awesome God, keeping covenant and steadfast love with those who love you and keep your commandments, we have sinned and done wrong, acted wickedly and rebelled, turning aside from your commandments and ordinances ... All Israel has transgressed your law and turned aside, refusing to obey your voice ... O Lord, in view of all your righteous acts, let your anger and wrath, we pray, turn away from your city Jerusalem, your holy mountain; because of our sins and the iniquities of our ancestors, Jerusalem and your people have become a disgrace among all our

> neighbours ... O Lord, hear; O Lord, forgive; O Lord, listen and act and do not delay! For your own sake, O my God, because your city and your people bear your name!" (Daniel 9:4-19).

Hear again words of John Saunders in 1838.

> Our influence has been deeply fatal to the black. It might have been supposed, that a Christian nation colonizing the Australian wilderness would have sought to bless the original possessor of the wild; but so far from this, we have inflicted a series of wrongs, which I will now enumerate.
>
> First, we have robbed him without any sanction, that I can find either in natural or revealed law; we descended as invaders upon his territory and took possession of the soil. It is not just to say that the natives had no notion of property, and therefore we could not rob them of that which they did not possess; for accurate information shews that each tribe had its distinct locality, and each superior person in the tribe a portion of this district. From these their hunting grounds, they have been individually and collectively dispossessed.
>
> We have also destroyed their game, and the fine-spun arguments about wild animals are adduced to show that the kangaroo and the opossum are the property of him who first obtains them. But apply this argument to the aristocratic privilege of Britain, and it ceases to hold good; the lord of the manor could transport a man, exile him from his country, his family, and friends, for

shooting a pheasant or snaring a hare; and the ground and the game, the sustenance and life of the New Hollander could be taken without compunction, or the offer of an equivalent. Surely we are guilty here.

Secondly, we have brutalised them. We brought the art of intoxication to them – we taught them new lessons in fraud, dishonesty, and theft … .

Thirdly, we have shed their blood. I speak not of the broils and murders which might find a parallel in the conduct of the white toward the white, but out of those extra murders in which so many have fallen. We have not been fighting with a natural enemy, but have been eradicating the possessors of the soil, and why, forsooth? because they were troublesome, because some few had resented the injuries they had received, and then how were they destroyed? by wholesale, in cold blood; let the Hawkesbury and Emu Plains tell their history, let Bathurst give in her account, and the Hunter render her tale, not to mention the South, and we shall find that while rum, and licentiousness, and famine, and disease, have done their part to exterminate the blacks, the musket, and the bayonet and the sword, and the poisoned damper, have also had their influence and that Britain hath avenged the death of her sons, not by law, but by retaliation at the atrocious disproportion of a hundred to one. The spot of blood is upon us, the blood of the poor and the defenceless, the blood of the men we wronged before we slew, and too, too often, a hundred times too often, innocent blood.

We may still feel that as we did not commit the great sins of breaking several of the Ten Commandments: "You shall not kill," "You shall not steal," "You shall not covet," that we should not have to repent.

But the Bible warns us that the sign of God's wrath is not only that people commit gross sins, but also approve of those who commit gross sins:

> Full of envy, murder, strife, deceit, craftiness, they are gossips, slanderers, God-haters, insolent, haughty, boastful, inventors of evil, rebellious toward parents, foolish, faithless, heartless, ruthless. They know God's decree, that those who practise such things deserve to die – yet they not only do them but even applaud others who practise them (Romans 1:30-32).

Others coveted, stole and killed, and we still benefit from their actions. Even if we did not do the original actions, many of us complied with the policy of Assimilation, which, even if well-intentioned, was so destructive to the social structures of Indigenous communities, as well as causing immense personal suffering. We still today benefit from those original sins. If we do not acknowledge that these were indeed sins, then we approve of what they did, and are complicit in their actions. A seared moral conscience, that does not acknowledge the presence of gross sin, is a sign of spiritual hardness of heart. And repentance must lead to recompense.

4. It is time to make recompense.

If I have hurt someone, it is not enough to be sorry, not even enough to repent. I must also recompense the person, or else my repentance is shown to be a sham.

The idea of recompense is not popular today, but it is essential. If I steal someone's car, then repent, I must return the car. If I steal someone's car, and smash it, and repent, I should buy the person another car. It is just common sense, and without it, we are not people of integrity.

Payment of recompense was required under the Law of Moses, namely five oxen for one ox, and four sheep for one sheep (Exodus 22:1). In the Gospels Zacchaeus is regarded as exemplary in his conversion, because his repentance was evident and public in his promise of recompense to those he had oppressed:

> Zacchaeus stood there and said to the Lord, "Look, half of my possessions, Lord, I will give to the poor; and if I have defrauded anyone of anything, I will pay back four times as much" (Luke 19:8).

What of practical Christian teaching on this matter? Richard Baxter, a Puritan minister of the 17th Century, wrote extensively on the duties of Christians in his *Christian Directory*. In Chapter XXXII, he wrote of "Cases and Directions about Satisfaction and Restitution." Here are some of his comments on the common duty of believers to provide satisfaction and restitution when they hurt others.

> Restitution is of the same thing which is taken away. Satisfaction is something different, for compensation or loss, but of equal value or use to the receiver. We should

provide restitution, but if not possible, satisfaction.

Who is bound to make Restitution and Satisfaction?

Every one that possesseth and retaineth that which is indeed another man's, and hath acquired no just title to it, must make restitution.

Those that concur in the injury, being accessories, are bound to satisfy.

To whom made?

To the true owner, if that cannot be, then to his heirs, who are the possessors of that which was his.
[In the case of murder] The Damage of heirs, kindred and creditor, must be repaired to the offender's estate.

He then gives some useful directions.

Foresee the trouble of restitution, and prevent it. Take heed of covetousness, which would draw you in such a snare.

Do nothing which is doubtful, if you can avoid it, lest it should put you to the trouble of Restitution.

When really you are bound to restitution or satisfaction, stick not at the cost or suffering, be it never so great, but be sure to deal faithfully with God and conscience.

If you are otherwise unable to satisfy, offer your labour

as a servant to him whom you are indebted ..."
(1990, pp. 896-898).

Of course we cannot earn our forgiveness from God. Forgiveness of any sin is always a free gift, given to us by our God of grace through the atoning death and resurrection of the Lord Jesus Christ. Restitution, satisfaction, recompense are not ways to earn forgiveness, but are signs of true repentance. They are signs of costly grace, rather than cheap grace (Bonhoeffer 1964, pp. 35-47). The scandal of God's free grace is that he even forgives theft and murder. But Christ's blood, though it makes us clean, does not remove the duty of restitution and recompense to those we have harmed.

As early as 1832, two Quakers, Backhouse and Walker, urged the British Government to return 20% of the land to the Aborigines, to no effect at that time (in World Vision Australia 2009, p. 11).

As Saunders preached in 1838,

> Then it is at once our duty, and our wisdom to humble ourselves in penitence before God. But repentance supposes reformation, and where injuries have been inflicted it involves recompense ... But the next step to reformation is restitution. And do we start at this word? It is one an honest man need never shrink from; it is one a noble mind will never discard; it is one which religious man will cheerfully adopt. It is our duty to recompense the Aborigines to the extent we have injured them.

We European Australians often claim that one of the strengths of the Australian character is 'caring for the underdog'. That claim is rank and blatant hypocrisy. We do not act with justice, let alone care.

I recognise that some people have done their best to care for Indigenous people, and to remedy wrongs. I recognise that some Christians have also done their best to remedy wrongs, to care for Indigenous people, and to share the gospel of Jesus Christ.

Thankfully there have also been efforts to provide some sort of recompense. The Aboriginal Protection Act of the Queensland government of 1897 aided the provision of Reserves. The recent Mabo judgement of 1992 and Native Title Act of 1993 has enabled some repossession of land, especially in northern Australia. In some parts of Australia there has been a policy of securing pastoral lease or freehold land for it to be owned and controlled by native title holders. These are encouraging first steps: I think that a more drastic act of recompense is required. (See Harris 1998, pp. 429-496 for background to land rights).

5. Recompense: A practical proposal

What might recompense, or what Baxter called *satisfaction*, require of us who arrived since 1788?

- We would recognise that recompense is a duty and responsibility, that we owe it to the Indigenous peoples of this land, out of respect for them as our brothers and sisters made in God's image, and out of awareness of the vileness of the crimes which have been committed against them and their ancestors.

- We would recognise that recompense is based on our

duty, not the needs of Indigenous people. I am not saying that we should not care, but that we must act with integrity and justice.

- We would recognise that no recompense could ever be satisfactory, because what was done was so vile, so immense, so universal, so pervasive, so destructive, so devastating, and so irreparable.

- We would ask the Indigenous people if they wanted those of us who have arrived since 1788 to leave [Baxter's *Restitution*], or to provide an equivalent recompense [Baxter's *Satisfaction*]. Leaving would be a drastic and complicated action, but, as I have pointed out, it has happened in India, Africa, and Indonesia in the last sixty years.

- If we do not leave, then we would need to ask each of the Indigenous peoples of this land what kind of recompense would be appropriate for them. This would be an extremely complicated and extensive task, but must done.

- We would need to be prepared to give costly recompense, lest it trivialise what has happened.

- We would then need to adopt a national recompense policy, in the form of a Treaty. It would need to be implemented locally, according to the wishes of each Indigenous tribe.

- By negotiation, it could be a one-off act of recompense, or it could be a constant and long-term series of acts of recompense.

- We could also implement voluntary recompense by churches in a coordinated way and should include support of Indigenous Christian ministry and training, as negotiated by the leaders of Christ's Indigenous people. Christian churches should lead the way in this, not least in supporting Indigenous Christians and their ministries. For churches, too, have benefited from the land they use and from income from those who have usurped the land.

It would be difficult to agree to do this, complicated to negotiate, and costly and demanding to deliver. The alternative is to fail in our moral duty, to admit that, for Australia, in Martin Luther King's words, "the bank of justice is bankrupt" (1963). We owe the Indigenous people of Australia not only their full rights as citizens of our nation, but also recompense for the damage we have done. Recognising citizenship and recognition of Native Title are just the first steps in a long process of appropriate restitution and recompense.

The idea of recompense is not alien to our society. As one well-known example, James Hardie, has had to provide recompense to workers harmed by working with asbestos. There is widespread feeling that this is right. If this recompense is right, then it is also right to offer recompense to the Indigenous people of Australia.

Ernest Gribble, a son of John Gribble, and also a worker among Indigenous people said:

> We have a three-fold debt to pay to the Aborigines.

> We owe them a debt for the country we have taken from them. We owe the race reparation for the neglect and cruelty ... We owe them the best our civilization has to give, and that is the gospel of our Lord (Harris in Dickey 1994, pp. 136,137).

It is time to pay our debts, for Paul writes:

> Owe no one anything, except to love one another; for the one who loves another has fulfilled the law. The commandments, "You shall not commit adultery; You shall not murder; You shall not steal; You shall not covet;" and any other commandment, are summed up in this word, "Love your neighbour as yourself." Love does no wrong to a neighbour; therefore, love is the fulfilling of the law (Romans 13:8-10).

Love involves duty as well as charity. We have wronged our neighbours. It is now time to pay our debts, to confess our sins, to give the recompense that we owe. We who know God's great love in Christ should be the most active in loving others. May God strengthen us to love the Lord our God, and so to love our neighbours.

References

Baxter, R. (1990). *A Christian directory: The practical works of Richard Baxter* (Vol. I). Ligonier: Soli Deo Gloria Publications. (It was written in 1664-1665, and first published in 1701).

Bonhoeffer, D. (1964). *The cost of discipleship.* London: SCM Press.

Calvin, J. (1997). *Sermons on Galatians* [Kathy Childress, Transl.]. Edinburgh: The Banner of Truth Trust.

Dickey, B. (1994). *The Australian dictionary of evangelical biography.* Sydney: Evangelical History Association.

Harris, J. (1998). *We wish we'd done more.* Adelaide: Openbook Publishers.

Lewis, C.S. (1964). *The discarded image.* Cambridge, UK: Cambridge University Press.

King, Jr. Martin Luther. *I have a dream.* A speech delivered at the march on Washington, DC, on August 28, 1963.

Saunders Revd J. *Claims of the Aborigines.* A sermon preached at Bathurst Street Baptist Church, Sydney, 14 October 1838.

Seiffert, M. (2008). *Refuge on the Roper: The origins of Roper River Mission Ngkurr*, Brunswick East, Victoria: Acorn Press.

Willison, G.F. (1964). *Saints and strangers.* New York: Time Life Books.

World Vision Australia (2009, July). Does Australia need a Treaty with its Indigenous people? *Faith and Life*, 10-11.

ANTIDOTE FOR A POISONED PLANET? THE CASE FOR RETHINKING STEWARDSHIP

Helen Beazley

The pre-eminence of the stewardship motif

Action-oriented Creation stewardship is gaining traction in churches, parachurch organisations and international church networks. Evangelical Christians all over the world have returned to the Genesis 2 account of Creation and the responsibility God gives humans to take care of our Garden (Genesis 2:15).[1]

Creation stewardship marks the key response of the evangelical Church as it awakens to the immensity of the crisis faced by the environment, taken to the brink by arrogant, unfettered, soulless consumption and an economic system whose mantra is growth at all costs. The church has come to terms with how largely unchallenged beliefs and paradigms have been nurturing unsustainable practices in energy production, agriculture, resource extraction, and manufacturing. And finally the church acknowledges that climate change heads a list of planet-threatening environmental consequences, which also includes accelerated species extinction, depletion of oil and other finite resources, loss of topsoil and soil fertility, loss of habitat, water scarcity, overfishing, pollution by toxins, and agricultural run off.

---

[1] In this essay, unless otherwise stated, Scripture taken from the Holy Bible, NEW INTERNATIONAL VERSION®. Copyright © 1973, 1978, 1984 by Biblica, Inc. All rights reserved worldwide. Used by permission.

Does this overstate the church's changing attitude? Well, at least parts of the evangelical church are heading in the right direction. One could argue that the 21st Century ends the unfettered reign of the priestly Creation Story – recorded in Genesis 1 and written about 500 years after the Yahwistic account found in Genesis 2-3 (Tubbs 1994). Simplistic renderings of the priestly Creation mandate to dominate the earth are an embarrassment to many Christians in these days of multiple impending environmental disasters and unsustainable population growth. The command to look after the earth in the Yahwistic account seems far more in step with the needs of our planet. In truth, the stewardship paradigm is the attempt of Bible scholars to harmonise both Creation stories.

Creation stewardship has shaped my understanding of the Christian's role towards the environment. It reaffirms the authority of the Bible and provides inspiration for an active response to the calamities that befall us.

With my feet firmly planted in the Creation stewardship camp, I found it unsettling to discover that some, like Steve Douglas, consider the stewardship ethic as "the most conservative, least evolved and least ecologically informed variant of Christian environmentalism," further maligned through being associated "with the more fundamentalist forms of Christianity" (2009, p. 721). While more generous in her assessment, Dorothy McDougall says "there are limits to its usefulness since the stewardship model continues to promote an anthropocentric worldview" (2003 p. 55) and further, "the stewardship model remains wedded to the old cosmological paradigm with its hierarchical, dualistic, patriarchal framework (p. 67).

Christians need a God-centred, rich, deep, compelling, enabling Bible narrative to motivate, mobilise and sustain active and effective engagement in the issues and solutions to environmental catastrophe. This essay explores whether the ethic of Creation stewardship is indeed robust enough to dismantle centuries of self-serving Biblical interpretations, and absorption of secular culture and ideologies that have disfigured the way people of faith have related to the environment.

I also make some tentative Scripture-centred reflections that embrace, but do not end with Creation stewardship as a way to begin reshaping our relationship with Creation. What the earth needs now is not more lords over Creation, but a scripturally supported, servanthood and reconciliation focused spirituality.

While this essay is positioned within evangelical traditions, I do draw on writers outside this tradition whose critiques of Western culture, influences in and on Christendom, and particular readings of the Bible help us re-engage with the Scriptures with greater wisdom, sensitivity and integrity. And while this essay does unsettle the view that stewardship is the best and most complete expression of our relationship with Creation, I also acknowledge our debt to those stewardship advancing theologians, scholars and writers (including Diane Jacobson, Theodore Hiebert, Douglas Hall, James B. Tubb, and Richard Young whose writings have informed this essay) who have broadened and enriched our understanding of what stewardship can mean, wrestling it away from narrow utilitarian notions. All the scriptural claims in this essay must be considered tentative, as we must always be cautious when taking our ancient sacred text, with particular meanings for ancient peoples, and trying apply it to our preoccupations and problems thousands of years later.

Stewardship: the cornerstone of the evangelical environmental response

Many Bible translators have rendered the Greek word *oikonomos* as 'steward'. Steward defines the role of looking after another's wealth and possessions and has been historically used to describe roles very divergent in social position – from the importance of a governor of a colonised people group to the more humble position of butler.

The concept of stewardship has become the accepted way of encapsulating our obligation to wisely use the things that God has gifted us with – whether it is possessions, money, talents, spiritual gifts, or Creation. We have inherited this concept from Christians who have gained their inspiration from Jesus' parables involving master – steward relationships, which are usually interpreted as positioning God as the owner of a household and humans as the household manager or steward.

The metaphor has been extended to describe our role in Creation, arising from a particular reading of Scripture. McDougall (2003, p. 47) asserts that connecting Creation with stewardship arose in the 1960s "as a model of ecological theology as a response to Lynn White's challenging indictment of Christianity and its historical relationship to global ecological decline." White's acerbic essay put Christendom on the back foot, outraged many Christians, but received the applause of many others, when he suggested that a particular reading of the Bible which had gained dominance in the West was in large part responsible for the contemptuous slash and burn environmental ethos of

Western society (White 1967).

The Bible never directly applies *oikonomos* to our relationship with nature. But while the household manager/caretaker/steward is not a Creation metaphor explicitly used in Scriptures, it does seem to aptly describe the relationship between God, humans and the rest of Creation when harmonising God's Genesis commands for dominion and caretaking.

Matthew 25:14-30, the parable of the talents (along with the parable of the minas in Luke 16), is frequently interpreted as an exhortation to be a good manager of the gifts God has given (although there is a strong case for a diametrically opposed interpretation of the passage as a critique of exploitative economic practices of the time). Interestingly this most celebrated narrative of stewardship does not use *oikonomous* but *doulos* – slave, to describe the recipient of the master's resources.

So how is this concept of Christian stewardship applied in the context of our present day environmental crisis? Stewardship is an apparently uncontentious rallying point for 21st Century Christians who are urged to swap the ethic of consumerism with the ethic of caretaking. Instead of seeing Creation as the raw material from which 'stuff' is made for us to buy, stewardship calls us to become aware of the enormous strain the earth is under, and return to the Genesis 2 command to care for the earth – often manifested in lifestyle changes to reduce energy and raw material use.

Locating the stewardship ethic within dominant cultural, ideological and theological discourses within the church

It seems so easy – deceptively easy – all we need to do is embrace stewardship, an undeniable, uncontroversial and benign concept, to empower and energise the church in taking up an environmental mission.

However, the significance of the Creation narrative has historically held a weak position in the range of preoccupations of the evangelical church. Some of these preoccupations even distort and misrepresent stewardship so that the stewardship paradigm itself becomes infused with unhelpful associations that reduce its legitimacy and capacity to rejuvenate our thinking about Creation. The major competing beliefs and sometimes obsessions can be summarised as follows.

The focus on the personal. An almost exclusive emphasis on personal piety, spiritual health, and fulfilment, has diminished the local church's readiness to engage with global issues.

The church's main vocation. At the top of the church's list of vocations is converting individuals to Christianity. Care for the environment has virtually no capacity for making converts. Social justice might be seen as less important than evangelism, but at least there is some scope to save souls when working with the impoverished.

At the level of meaning making, this also represents a suppression of the Creation story as *a key* to understanding God and our relationship with Him, usurped by the redemption narrative that has become *the only authoritative key* to understanding God and our relationship to Him. Just as an 'other-worldly' preoccupation has diminished our ability to take action on social issues, it also leaves the church unprepared, defensive and scrabbling for deep Biblical wisdom to inform its conversation with society about ecological redemption.

In engaging the evangelical church in the work of ecological recovery, a central enterprise for evangelical theologians will be to rehabilitate the story of Creation from its current undervalued status, so that the Creation narrative and the story of Jesus can sit side by side and be viewed as complementary as they speak to the revelation, incarnation and heart of God.

Sinfulness of the physical world. Misinterpretation of Bible passages such as Christians not being of the world (e.g. John 17:16) leads to the unhelpful conclusion that the physical world is corrupt and to be withdrawn from.

Debilitating eschatologies. Passionate views about the coming destruction of this heaven and earth and the creation of a new heaven and earth leads to shoulder shrugging fatalism and inaction.

Separatism. Stemming from the early days of the Western environmental movement where many were inspired by Eastern religious thought and nature worship (think James Cameron's *Avatar*), there remains a sense that being involved in the environmental movement gives tacit approval to, and may pollute evangelical Christianity with, pantheistic sentiments.

Outside Western discourses. There are also ideologies and patterns of thought that have no origin in Christian thought or

Scripture, but hold sway in the Christian psyche and church culture. These include:

- The Platonic world view, tainting Christian theology since early times, that separates the physical and spiritual, with the physical world inferior to the spiritual, and by logical extension unworthy of our care.

- Scientific methodologies from the 16th Century onwards which taught us to objectify nature as something separate from us, to be observed, manipulated and controlled.

- An uncritical belief in the march of human progress fuelled by scientific discovery, including an unfettered optimism that science (and not behaviour change) will find a way out of any messes we make.

- A love affair with rising living standards, and 'stuff'.

Thomas Berry calls the dysfunctional outcome of this confluence of Western beliefs a type of "cultural autism" where our culture cannot even grapple with the kinds of transformations in our collective thinking necessary to avert global disaster (Berry in McDougall 2003 p. 16).

As we will see, all of these influences have had their role muting, blunting and at worst hijacking and perverting the stewardship motif.

Breaking it down

Before engaging with the criticisms of stewardship by Douglas and others we need to deconstruct its constituent claims.

- God made everything, but Creation is separate from God.

- Everything belongs ultimately to God but God has given humans dominion.

- Humans are given a special role over Creation as stewards.

- Gifts given to us are to be used wisely, in accordance with God's will.

The remainder of this essay examines these beliefs; tests their robustness against the Scriptural record, their ability to advance the cause of Christian environmentalism and how well they stand up against competing preoccupations of the evangelical church; and suggests ways of reshaping these perspectives to develop a stronger, more comprehensive and integral framework for action.

I draw on both scholars outside of the evangelical tradition who provide a useful role in critiquing the weaknesses of stewardship (even though their conclusions and alternative visioning of ecological theology may be unacceptable to most evangelicals) and evangelical scholars whose work has provided correctives to unhelpful, fundamentalised interpretations of the stewardship motif.

The source of the sacred

Paradigm problems

Our Creation story obliges us, and liberates us, to view God separate from His Creation. This is in total distinction to pantheism, which sees unpredictable gods inhabiting living and non-living things, and panentheism, where Creation is part of, but not completely, God.

Does this mean that with the exception of humans, nature is devoid of God?

Lynn White's controversial 1966 address (published in 1967) *The Historical Roots of Our Ecological Crisis* claimed the dominant form of Christianity provided the philosophical base for plundering the earth. Often misunderstood as anti-Christian, White believed that by stripping away God from Creation because of its emphasis on separating God from His Creation, the Western formulation of Christianity was responsible for ecological disaster.

> In Antiquity every tree, every spring, every stream, every hill had its own genius loci, its guardian spirit. These spirits were accessible to men, but were very unlike men; centaurs, fauns, and mermaids show their ambivalence. Before one cut a tree, mined a mountain, or dammed a brook, it was important to placate the spirit in charge of that particular situation, and to keep it placated. By destroying pagan animism, Christianity made it possible to exploit

nature in a mood of indifference to the feelings of natural objects (p. 4).

The spirits in natural objects, which formerly had protected nature from man, evaporated. Man's effective monopoly on spirit in this world was confirmed, and the old inhibitions to the exploitation of nature crumbled (p. 5).

When it comes to humans, Christians are constantly called to see God in the other. As humans are made in the image of God they have a sacred value. We are invited to see Jesus in the lives of those experiencing injustice or misfortune in the parable of the sheep and goats (Matthew 25). But because of the absence of the *Imago Dei* (image of God) in all but humans, and anxieties around returning to nature worship, even perhaps the fear of being constrained from doing as we please to nature, we are hardened to those Scriptures which see God in intimate relationship with non-human nature. We are very reluctant to see that boundaries might be blurred, and that while God is not nature (pantheism), and nature is not part of the substance of God (panentheism), yet He has a ponderous, ongoing, intimate relationship with Creation.

As mentioned previously, our resistance to entangling nature and the spirit of God also has its roots in the Reformation where salvation and our heavenly destiny trumps any other Biblical narrative, viewing Creation as at best a scenic backdrop to the main drama, at worst fallen and evil with nothing of value to add to the story arc. Hence, the streets of gold in the hereafter edge out the forests of green in the here and now as the revelation of God's purposes.

We have also been misled by the modern scientific discourse that has, by relegating nature to the status of a 'thing' to be observed and manipulated, dis-enchanted and de-sacrelised Creation.

Revitalising the paradigm: sacrelising Creation

God's intimate knowing and sustaining of nature is recognised in the Epistles.

> For from him and through him and to him are all things (Romans 11:36).

> [Jesus] is before all things, and in him all things hold together (Colossians 1:7).

> ... and there is but one Lord, Jesus Christ, through whom all things came and through whom we live (1 Corinthians 8:6).

We also know that God imprinted His character on Creation.

> The heavens declare the glory of God; the skies proclaim the work of his hands (Psalm 19:1).

> For since the creation of the world God's invisible qualities – his eternal power and divine nature – have been clearly seen, being understood from what has been made, so that men are without excuse (Romans 1:20).

Some, like Catholic missionary and teacher Vincent Donovan (1989 p. 129) go as far as to say, "We must come, at last, to understand that our primary revelation is creation, the unwritten book, as sacred as any published one." While Evangelicals might feel uncomfortable giving Creation the same status as the Bible, we must learn to elevate Creation's revelatory power – it is not mere scenery but bears God's imprint that eons of human generations have marvelled at and through which have known something of God.

We know that Creation brings joy to God and satisfies His creativity.

> God saw all that he had made, and it was very good (Genesis 1:31).

We also know that God has chosen all of Creation to be redeemed.

> For the creation was subjected to frustration, not by its own choice, but by the will of the one who subjected it, in hope that the creation itself will be liberated from its bondage to decay and brought into the glorious freedom of the children of God (Romans 8: 20-21).

Finally, we know that God is praised by nature.[2]

> Praise him, sun and moon, praise him, all you shining stars (Psalm 148:3).

Together, these passages highlight God's ongoing, sustaining,

---

[2] Famous chimpanzee researcher Jane Goodall describes as "awe" the behaviour of a chimpanzee she observed when encountering a waterfall. She interpreted his ecstatic dancing and other behaviours as a primitive religious experience (Goodall 1971). Could such behaviours among non-human sentient creatures be a form of unselfconscious praise to our God?

intimate, present, and indwelling relationship with the community of Creation, which affirms His own character, and is the pinnacle of the outworking of His creativity. Arguably, not only does Creation reveal God's attributes to us, it provides self-revelation, demonstrating God's capacity for wondrousness and magnificence and intricacy to Himself. While God is not Creation, we may need to accept that the mechanics of the intimate relationship God has with non-human Creation remains part of the glorious mystery of God not yet fully revealed to us.

Embracing the sanctity and mystery of nature as belonging to, and a form of worship to, God, can also lead to a reworking of human identity. Thomas Berry describes humans as the "celebratory species" – the species blessed with the gift of conscious self-awareness which enables us, in the service of all of Creation, to understand the enormous wonder of all species and celebrate and praise God for His marvelous works (in McDougall 2003, p. 119).

We must re-evaluate again the views of Christian writers considered pantheists or panentheists, against Scriptures, to make sure we have not dismissed them too lightly. While such writers may phrase the problem in language that is dangerously pantheistic, we must take note of their concern that (in language more acceptable to our evangelical sentiments), we have lost the immanent, present God of the Scriptures in favour of perhaps a more comfortable image of a transcendent God. Comfortable, because a transcendent God will be less concerned about the way we deal with the rest of Creation.

Converting our hearts

In response to an immanent God intimately concerned and affectionately bound to what He has made, our weighty obligation must be to affirm that non-human Creation, like human Creation, is sacred.

But what does it mean to understand Creation as 'sacred' and what would the outworking of a wholehearted conviction followed by conscientious action look like?

'Sacred' denotes something belonging to, devoted or dedicated to God, and as a result afforded great honour and reverence. Attached to the meanings of sacred is also the concept of taboos – what can or cannot be done to something because it is sacred. Sacrelising Creation in our hearts, and acting on this with conviction, revolutionises our relationship with Creation, throwing up all sorts of new possibilities in the way we act towards nature. For example:

- Shouldn't it be taboo to destroy an animal or plant species, directly or indirectly, when each life form has been made by and is sacred to God?

- Shouldn't it be taboo to destroy entire habitats because less of Creation is available to demonstrate to all people groups and future generations the character of God, one of the fundamental ways God has chosen to reveal Himself?

- Isn't planting a tree or creating a frog habitat in backyards as important as prayer, vocal praise and financial giving as a sacred act of worship – dedicating restored

Creation to the service of God? (We need to decide whether the Bible's references to non-human Creation praising God are merely a metaphorical devise or real acts of worship, and that restoring habitat is expanding the symphony of praise.)

- Isn't mindfulness of God's handiwork in the bush and/or on the footpath worthy of being a central spiritual discipline?

- Aren't protests against the destruction of nature acts of love and service which our Creator longs for?

- Isn't Christian indifference to Creation, indifference to its Maker, while love of Creation speaks of love of the Creator?

A strong sense of the sanctity of nature, and a determination to work this out in our culture and lifestyles, could powerfully constrain our impulse to take remorselessly from nature what we do not need and instead value Creation for what it tells us about God and for the pleasure and joy it gives our Creator.

Dethroning God's rival

Paradigm problems

Despite claims that the stewardship discourse is theocratic (God at the centre) many argue that the subtext of stewardship is that humans are in charge and – for some – only accountable to God for under-use of the resources He has put at our disposal.

The stewardship ethic holds together two Biblical narratives of possession. One is that the earth belongs to God as opposed to humans – a dominant theme in the Bible. The other is that the earth belongs to humans as opposed to other living things – a subordinate theme in the Bible.

The first narrative can be found in such passages as:

> The earth is the LORD's, and everything in it, the world, and all who live in it (Psalm 24:1).

> I have no need of a bull from your stall
> or of goats from your pens,
> for every animal of the forest is mine,
> and the cattle on a thousand hills.
> I know every bird in the mountains,
> and the creatures of the field are mine.

> If I were hungry I would not tell you,
> for the world is mine, and all that is in it (Psalm 50:9-11).

> The heavens are yours, and yours also the earth; you founded the world and all that is in it (Psalm 89:11,12).

Many Old Testament stories have been interpreted as God reinforcing His right to be in charge of the earth over the human impulse to be in charge. Examples include expulsion of Adam and Eve from the Garden of Eden (Genesis 3), the story of Noah (Genesis 6,7), the Tower of Babel (Genesis 11:1-8), and the exile.

This tussle between God and humans for rulership – underpinned by the legitimacy of God as ruler and the illegitimacy of humans in charge – is in fact fundamental to our

Christian cosmology, that is humanity's place in the universe. One significant understanding of sin in evangelical theology is our desire to dethrone God and be in charge, rather than submitting to His divine authority.

The second narrative, where God sanctions human control over the earth, can be found in:

- You made him ruler over the works of your hands; you put everything under his feet (Psalm 8:6).

- The highest heavens belong to the LORD, but the earth he has given to man (Psalm 115:16).

- and more prominently and famously in the Priestly Creation story.

    Then God said, "Let us make man in our image, in our likeness, and let them rule over the fish of the sea and the birds of the air, over the livestock, over all the earth, and over all the creatures that move along the ground

    So God created man in his own image,
    in the image of God he created him;
    male and female he created them.

    God blessed them and said to them, "Be fruitful and increase in number; fill the earth and subdue it. Rule over the fish of the sea and the birds of the air and over every living creature that moves on the ground." (Genesis 1:26-28).

The King James version features the well known translations of *radah* as "dominion" (vs 26, 28) and *kabas* as "subdue"" (vs 28). Other translations use the terms "complete authority over" (vs 26 Amplified) and "reign over" (vs 26 New Living Translation).

We inherit a strong theological tradition including the writings of such luminaries as Thomas Aquinas, Origen, Luther, Calvin, and Bath, which interprets such passages to mean that God has gifted humans with an absolute, dictatorial control over nature. For example:

> Luther, commenting upon humankind's expanded dominion (to eat meat) granted by God in Genesis 9:2-3, notes that it is a "more extensive and oppressive dominion" than existed before the fall and flood, that humans are given authority like that of "a tyrant who has absolute power" over life and death. This should "make our consciences relaxed and free" in using created things, as there is no divine law to forbid such usage and thus it is no sin. Indeed, God's gift of tyrannical dominion provides reliable and excellent proof that God "no longer hates man but is kindly disposed toward him" (Tubbs 1994, p. 545).

The view of ascendant humanity is strengthened by another theological discourse – the strong emphasis in Western Christian traditions of a transcendent God – that distorts into a Creator who distances Himself from non-human Creation. One theologian says of this historical tendency, "A stewardship theology that builds on a transcendent, deistic God undermines its own well-meaning program" (Jerry Robins in Young 1994, p. 101).

Revitalising the paradigm: Becoming the owner-Creator's butler

Many eco-theologians abandon any attempt to integrate *radah* and *kabas* into an understanding of humanity's role in the environment, believing that this anthropocentric concept fuels a dangerously arrogant and hostile relationship with the rest of Creation.

However, those of us who are committed to the Scriptures remain committed to reconciling the Maker and the apparent despot. We do this by seeing in the scriptural record the might and absolute control God has as creator, sustainer, omnipotent presence over all creation and at times supernatural intervener, against a partial authority afforded to humans.

False sense of power

The character of humanity's control of nature must be contextualised by the strong biblical statement that God, and God alone, is responsible for keeping the cosmos intact. If we believe the Bible, God is not the clockmaker that has set on the clock and then retreated from active involvement as the enlightenment philosophers came to believe. God must be present to sustain the universe – humans have absolutely no power to keep the universe operational. So human arrogance must stumble at the very first Creative principle – that without God's continuing creative activity all of Creation would perish. Humans would not be able to save themselves.

Highly conditional control

Casting our net broadly throughout the Bible, we find that there are four clear ways that the Scriptures undermine the view that God has afforded humans absolute control over the earth. Firstly God continues to be intimately involved in Creation. For example, astoundingly Jesus says that while valued so little by humans, God knows and cares for each sparrow (Matthew 10:29, Luke 12:6).

Secondly, the Old Testament contains numerous injunctions where God limits the control and decision making humans can have over nature, most notably in not eating from the tree of knowledge of good and evil, many other dietary laws, jubilee laws limiting production and property accumulation, helping animals in particular situations, and tithing (Tubbs 1994, pp. 547-548). Original sin happened in the context of humans' overreach into a part of nature proscribed as off limits by God, with clear parallels today as we fail to observe taboos in our consumption of the environment, with curses resulting for humanity and nature.

Thirdly, our ongoing hold on the earth is somewhat tenuous, subject to obedience to God and consequently always under the threat of forfeiture. We find this both in the Garden of Eden and in the story of the Hebrews.

> Those who obeyed received all the blessings of life – well-being, prosperity, fruitfulness, security, and land – and those who disobeyed received a negation of life, whether by extermination, exile, barrenness, or natural disaster (Brueggemann 1997, p. 195).

Fourthly, the Bible teaches us to look to God for our needs to be met – recognising our ongoing dependence on God as Creator and provider rather than pride in our own resourcefulness to mercilessly extract from Creation. Scholars regard the manna story as teaching the Hebrews an alternative to Egyptian society, by placing restrictions on the excessive consumption of natural resources (Myers 2001, pp. 10-14), recalled by Jesus who teaches us to ask only for our daily bread.

Clothing ourselves in the servant motif

We can also draw on Biblical metaphors of governor and servant embedded in the political and economic domains of Bible times, to find parallels with our positional relationship to God. These have echoes in our own culture. *Radah* could imply kingdom, with humans as monarchs but more appropriately the word conveys governorship. God as ruler bestows on humans as governors certain responsibilities towards Creation. Within the governorship paradigm, as well as positional authority and responsibility, there is also obligation and accountability. A governor also has a representational role – made in the image of God, humans represent God on earth. One historical meaning of steward in fact, is an official who has a representative role in a country on behalf of a monarch, though steward is also historically used to mean a servant in charge role in an affluent household, that is a butler.

The managerial 'servant in charge/master' construct is used frequently through the Gospels to denote the relationship between God and humans. Matthew 18 is the parable of the unmerciful servant, Matthew 24 and Luke 12 tells of the servant who is on guard for his master's return and the one who is not, Matthew 25 contains the story of the servants entrusted with talents,[3] Luke 14 has the servant who collects the poor

---

[3] Later in this essay, the alternative view of the parable of the talents is discussed, where the master in not interpreted to represent God.

for the master's feast, while Luke 16 states that no servant has two masters.

We have acute difficulty in moving from a Psalm 8 'the earth is my footstool' mindset found in only a few Bible verses, to the far more pervasive servant/master relationship which honours God's absolute ownership and acknowledges that God puts limitations on our servant in charge role.

Challenging our ingrained psychic entitlement to land ownership

A significant mental barrier to acknowledging God's entitlement to the earth is the entanglement of our attitudes and Western property rights. Our laws and culture unrelentingly reinforce humans as possessors of the land while there is little to reinforce God as the owner in anything other than in a highly spiritualised form. Key characteristics of most types of Western land ownership are (1) people make a claim on land, (2) individuals rather than groups own land, (3) ownership responsibilities are tied to highly defined parcels of property, and (4) ownership and attendant responsibilities are for a finite period of time, passing to someone else through a monetary transaction or inheritance. It is hard to imagine any other aspect of our enculturation that does more to define ourselves as owners (rather than servants) who can buy and sell devoid of ongoing responsibility to care for the land, despite all our stewardly protestations that we are caretakers of the land we possess.

We must look outside current Western land ownership practices to understand that other relationships with the land exist. Leviticus 25 is where God's ideal of land ownership is documented. For 49 years the property market can operate, with land being bought and sold (operating similar to a lease), but no one family can build up an unchallenged property empire because in the 50th year land returns to the family to whom it was originally allocated. Families had enduring duties to the land.

Australian Aboriginal ways of relating to the land is another model in complete contradistinction to Western ways in that (1) the land makes claims on the people (the reverse of Western systems) (2) people groups rather than individuals have entitlements, (3) land is not tightly defined/bounded, and (4) responsibility is unending in time: "While holding strong ties through custodial responsibility for place, Indigenous peoples do not own place" (Lester 2008, p. 22).

According to customary Aboriginal law, as explained by a senior traditional lawman of the Ngarinyin people "I don't own the land, but the land owns me ... That's why it's important to us, because the land owns us" (in Gibson 2007, pp. 63-64). Gibson states:

> While conventional models of ownership vest, in the individual, rights with respect to a recognisable and exhaustible entity, diverse Indigenous concepts of custodianship resist the universality of this regime and suggest various relationships of shared and enduring interaction with the land that transcend each individual and indeed the 'boundary' of the parcel itself (p. 64).

As previously stated, many ecotheologians will never be happy with a theology that imparts any type of unique authority but the Scriptures leads us to this unavoidable conclusion. So how should we be present in Creation and escape our skewed, overwhelming sense of entitlement to the land, an entitlement which resonates so deeply in our collective psyches and poisons any possibility of a constructive relationship with the environment?

Stewardship must be redefined to lift up God as absolute and reconstruct the role of humanity as a humble servant who must observe limits. We must cling to the humblest metaphors that still resonate with our sacred text, that acknowledge the perverse outcomes when we act without restraint.

Converting our hearts

'Steward' as we have seen, can convey the meaning of a highly ranked official with governing authority over a country, or it can mean something more humble – like a butler with some limited and conditional control over parts of a household. Let's see ourselves as butlers who will never be confused with the owner of the house, rather than kings and queens with absolute rights.

We need to unshackle stewardship from the weighty handicap of arrogant anthropocentrism and move much further towards a theocratic underpinning or reject this metaphor in favour of something more benign – such as custodian or trustee.

For property owners perhaps it can start with our own relationship with our own land as purchased under the law. In Australia, we must first acknowledge that the soil that our home is erected on is stolen land so can never be truly ours. Next, we can think of how to maximise the value of the land for God, rather than maximising its value to ourselves.

This could mean keeping our houses small and restoring original vegetation. And instead of selling to the highest bidder, we could sell to the person who is most likely to look after the land in a way that brings most glory to God. Perhaps we should return our properties to the original owners and lease it back.

Foolish? It does seem crazy talk, but if we want to see a right relationship between God and humans and Creation expressed other than in Sunday liturgies, we need to have conversations about how to relinquish our devastating attitudes of control over Creation and enact humble servanthood toward our Creator-Owner and Creation.

Our current environmental crisis demands that we move away from our habitual grooves of a spirit-devoid Creation that deifies humans, towards the less familiar terrain of the sanctity of Creation and the ownership of God.

The beasts and the flowers fight back

The previous section argued that God has never relinquished his ownership of the world to human hands and that human control is partial and limited by God. A stewardship model can only be effective if it corrects our skewed and inflated sense of control. We now explore the other half of the 'chain of being' and the ways stewardship addresses our relationship with the rest of Creation.

Paradigm problems

Evangelicals claim our superior position over all other living things arises from the Priestly Creation account in Genesis 1 where humans are created as the pinnacle of Creation and, uniquely, in the image of God.

The centrality of humanity in Creation has been reinforced by a dominant theme in Greek philosophy which Christian writers point to as a strong influence in shaping the church's formative views about the place of the non-human world. Greek stoic Cicero asserts:

> Here somebody will ask, for whose sake was all this vast system contrived? For the sake of the trees and plants, for these, though without sensation, have their sustenance from nature? But this at any rate is absurd. Then for the sake of the animals? It is not more likely that the gods took all this trouble for the sake of dumb, irrational creatures. For whose sake then shall one pronounce the world to have been created? Doubtless for the sake of those living beings which have the use of reason. Thus we are led to believe that the world and all the things that it contains were made for the sake of gods and men (in Wilkinson 1991, p. 122).

And again, we must recognise a long tradition of influential theologians who took the Genesis 1 passage to express an extreme, hierarchical order to Creation.

Many ecotheologians find that locating humans above Creation rather than within Creation galling, another embarrassing ideological prop for the tyrannical abuse of nature. Ecofeminist theologians in particular find that church culture is loaded with forms of domination through condoning a 'hierarchy of existence' in relation to God (ultimate worth) and Creation (little worth), male (high worth) and female (low worth), human (high worth) and non-human (low worth). It is argued that these dualisms interplay, where God and male are aligned, and female and Creation (e.g. 'mother earth') are aligned, with God and male being assigned a higher intrinsic worth than female and Creation (McDougall 2003, pp. 28-29).

While the special position of humans in Creation is undeniable to those of us committed to the authority of Scriptures, the stewardship motif appears to progress linearly (from God to humans to the rest of Creation) rather than integrating an interdependent, co-operative vision of the relationship between human and non-human Creation despite much acknowledgement of mutuality in the Biblical record.

Revitalising stewardship: Our common ground

Strident confidence in human supremacy over all things living and non-living becomes more unsettled as we look at the beliefs supporting this confidence.

Image of God

Genesis 1:26 closely associates dominion with *imago Dei* – so that the verse is universally interpreted to mean that humanity's authority over nature comes from humanity being made in the image and likeness of God.

Then God said, "Let us make man in our image, in our

likeness, and let them rule over the fish of the sea and the birds of the air, over the livestock, over all the earth, and over all the creatures that move along the ground."

Biblical scholarship has however, opened up observations and interpretations that lead us to a humble and conditioned understanding of *imago Dei* and its implications for our responsibility to nature. Below are three distinct reflections on *imago Dei*.

Firstly, the *imago Dei* motif comes out of a background of slavery for the Hebrew people. The writer is emphasising that "their deepest identity was not rooted in their experience of slavery, but in their experience of the divine imprint upon their humanity" (McDougall 2003, p. 44).

Secondly, to express God's likeness in dominion, Biblical scholars like Diane Jacobson point out that we need to model ourselves on the person who most completely demonstrates the nature of God – Jesus Christ and his gracious, self-giving kingship. She says, "This dominion is marked by justice and concern, by care and radical service, even unto death" (in McDougall 2003, p. 45). Thirdly, Douglas John Hall traces the history of scholarship relating to *imago Dei* and finds that beside the "substantialist" view – that God's likeness is about some particular aspects of God indwelling humans – is another view found in the writings of Luther and Calvin, of *imago Dei* that sees our likeness to God coming from having a relationship to God so that we are only able to reveal God's image as we turn to, and are in right relationship with God. Hall explains:

> What is presupposed by this interpretation ... is quite

> simply the relationship between Creation and creature. The image of God is something that 'happens' as a consequence of this relationship. The human creature images (used as verb) its Creator because and insofar as
>
> it "turned toward" God. To be *imago Dei* does not mean to have something but to be and do something: to image God (1986, p. 98).

This reaffirms the call of Jacobson and others that to turn to God and being in the right relationship to Him will find its expression in a humble, servant like orientation to nature.

Repentance and reconciliation, not arrogance

Granting humans dominion occurred before the Fall, when humans in their sinless state could be trusted to understand and preserve the harmony of the Creation community that was a reflection of the unity and harmony of the triune Creator God (Young 1994, p. 62).

After the Fall, humans are no longer able to model God's relationship to Creation, instead discord characterises relationships in Genesis as a result of human sin and God's curses.

> No longer was there peace in God's creation: an animal was slain for clothing (3:21), Adam and Eve were banished from the garden (3:23), Cain slew Abel (4:8), the ground did not yield for Cain, who became a homeless wanderer (4:10-12), Lamech became a murderer (4:23), and the whole earth was filled with wickedness (6:5) (Young 1994, p. 71).

Nature continues to suffer from God's anger at human evil and sin.

> Therefore the earth will mourn
> and the heavens above grow dark,
> because I have spoken and will not relent,
> I have decided and will not turn back (Jeremiah 4:28).

Paul vividly describes the travail of Creation after the Fall.

> For the creation was subjected to frustration, not by its own choice, but by the will of the one who subjected it, in hope that the creation itself will be liberated from its bondage to decay and brought into the glorious freedom of the children of God (Romans 8: 20-21).

Repentance and a desire to restore Creation to reflect the unity and harmony of our Creator-God needs to conquer dangerous, willful abuse of our unique place in Creation. In this context, we should consider John Pawlikowski's contention that *reconciliation* should be "the primary paradigm" shaping our relationship to the earth (in McDougall 2003, p. 48). As ministers of reconciliation (2 Corinthians 5:18) we can extend our ministry to restoring the broken relationship between humans and Creation as a result of the Fall.

Service not servitude

The Yahwist story places humans within Creation, with animals as helpers, and a duty to till and to care. Some look to the more literal translation of *avad* being not 'to till', but 'to serve' as a bonded slave would serve.

> *Young's literal translation*: And Jehovah God taketh the man, and causeth him to rest in the garden of Eden, to serve it, and to keep it (Genesis 2:15).

Theodore Hiebert says:

> Moreover, the role assigned humans within creation in this story is not to rule (*radah*) and to subdue (*kavash*) but rather to 'serve' (*avad*; Genesis 2:15; 3:23). The Hebrew term *avad* is properly translated 'till' in these verses (NRSV), since it clearly refers to the cultivation of arable land. But *avad* is in fact the ordinary Hebrew verb 'serve', used of slaves serving masters and of humans serving God (Genesis 12:16; Exodus 4:23).

> The language with which the role of the human in the earth is described is not the language of lordship but of servanthood. In this account of creation, the theology of the human place in creation is not a theology of dominion but a theology of dependence (1996 http://www.directionjournal.org/article/?922).

This is a stunning counterpoint to a dominion theology. To consider ourselves as servants (or more strongly slaves) of Creation, supported by a more literal reading of Genesis 2:15, helps us develop an entirely new and energising relationship to Creation. Serving not only God but nature as well is a fitting attribute for followers of Jesus as ours is a faith characterised by servanthood.

Dependence and interdependence

One interpretation of the dominion verses of Genesis 1 and the caretaker verse of Genesis 2 is that non-human Creation is somehow dependent on humans for continued life. But there is no scriptural suggestion that humans are needed to keep ecosystems vibrant and robust.

In fact, quite the opposite, the Yahwist account makes clear humanity's dependence on Creation. We know from the places on earth uninhabited by humans, that humans are not an indispensable part of ecologies. On the other hand Genesis 2 finds God bringing together the elements of Creation needed by Adam to sustain him: God planted a garden with a river watering it, provided trees for food and aesthetics, and made animals which were helpers (not as a food source until Genesis 8). Adam is not brought to life until he is brought into the life-sustaining garden. Perhaps this dependence relationship can inform a re-reading of Genesis 1 – that humans were not created last as the apex of Creation but last because of humans' utter dependence on the rest of Creation, Creation as a whole sustained by God.

If Adam and Eve's work is interpreted as 'to till' it makes sense that they must also 'care'. This seems like an acknowledgement that when humans must modify their environment for production, they have a responsibility to care for the environment given the tendency for degradation where human activity is involved. When humans must rescue increasingly unviable ecosystems, it is because their activities have violated the integrity of ecosystems in the first place.

It is worth remembering that each living thing is dependent on the creative acts of other living things – God has endowed all living things (not just humans) with the ability to re-create the species and create to the benefit of others. The most important life-giving creative act does not come from humans but from plant life. Plants use the sun's energy to break the bonds of carbon dioxide, releasing oxygen to fuel photosynthesis that enables plants to grow, flower and fruit. Without the God-made life giving processes of plants, there would be no food chain and humans would not be able to exist.

Our common life

Bible scholars find much in the Scriptures that point to our common experience. We are all created by God, with humans sharing the 6th day with animals; and plants, animals and humans are made from the same earth (Genesis 2:19). We share the miraculous breath of God that animates humans and animals (Ecclesiastes 3:19). All living things are mortal "All people are grass ... The grass withers, the flower fades" (Isaiah 40:6-8; 1 Peter 1:24) and the bodies of all things return to the earth in death. We together suffer the results of God's curses, for example human and non-human Creation both suffered during the flood. The Noahic Covenant includes all life (Genesis 8:21). In the New Testament, the story of redemption through Christ has both a human and non-human dimension, the "whole creation" will be freed (Romans 8:19-22) (Tubbs 1994, pp. 548-549).

Converting our hearts

The Bible evidences the commonality and communion humans have with nature. The Bible gives credence to Thomas Berry's saying "The universe is a community of subjects, not a collection of objects" (in McDougall 2003, p. 65).

Positioning humans as the pinnacle of Creation, and consequently subordinating all other living things has been a constant worry to many ecology minded Biblical scholars. Anthropocentrism so easily slips into uncaring, dismissive, and dictatorial treatment of non-human Creation.

Moderating any haughtiness arising from our unique position in Creation is the recognition of our utter dependence on nature, our obligations to serve Creation, our common history and destiny with the rest of Creation, and recognition that God's redemptive grace extends to all elements of Creation.

Praise for the indolent

Paradigm problems

The conventional meaning of stewardship presumes an active and productive economic role for the steward. Stewardship is a "doing" motif. The King's steward must secure the wealth and possessions of the king; the Lord's butler must keep his/her master's house in order.

The stewardship ethic when applied to Creation also infers an economic role for humans: where human activity and the environment combine to produce something useful to humans and pleasing to God. Genesis 2 observes that before God creates humans there is no one to work the ground. The parable of the talents appears to commend only those servants that put the master's money to work to multiply its value.

Taken to its extreme, stewardship is seen as condoning (or at least having little to say about) the worldview that constructs the environment solely as an exclusive gift to humans, and principally raw materials to be used (and must be used) to increase our standard of living. Critics of stewardship label this as an 'instrumental', 'utilitarian' or 'productionist' view of Creation – in other words valuing Creation only as an instrument for advancing human interests and forcing to the margins other ways of valuing the environment.

Revitalising stewardship: Challenging utilitarianism

Stewardship can be reformed when we ask the question, if we have a special role in Creation as God's representatives, what are God's purposes for Creation that we are to co-operate with in fulfilling our role.

God provides for the entire Creation community

Of course, part of God's purpose for Creation is to provide for the needs of humans for water, food and shelter. However, God is providential to the whole of the Creation community, with all living things having their needs met through an interdependent web – God is concerned, but not only concerned, with meeting human needs.

> Then God said [to humans], "I give you every seed-bearing plant on the face of the whole earth and every tree that has fruit with seed in it. They will be yours for food. And to all the beasts of the earth and all the birds of the air and all the creatures that move on the ground – everything that has the breath of life in it – I give every green plant for food." And it was so (Genesis 1:29-30).

Surprisingly, God is able to turn nothing, or barren wilderness, into places of plenty, as demonstrated in the Garden of Eden and the Hebrews' 40 year wilderness experience. In contrast our overuse and abuse of Creation can turn places of plenty into barrenness.

Rereading the parable of the talents

When interviewed for the BBC Channel 4 documentary *God is Green*, Bill Raney, CEO of West Virginia Coal Association, evangelical Christian and believer in stewardship, was asked whether his company's highly polluting mountain topping extraction practices were exploiting rather than caring for Creation. He replied, "I think it would be very wasteful for us to neglect the use of resources that have been put in the earth" and confirmed he believed that God has put the coal there for humans to use (Dowd 2007).

Raney's comment represents the views of many in the church who either understand stewardship to mean, or believe stewardship easily complements the view, that God gifted us with an environment to consume in the interests of human development and standard of living, and not to use would be to waste. In fact, in this formulation of stewardship 'any use' is better in bringing glory to God (regardless of the environmental consequences) than 'no use'.

The parable of the talents has been traditionally used in the pulpit to connect stewardship with productivity and to exhort Christians to passionately put to use the gifts God has endowed us with. We are to emulate the two enterprising servants who multiply the wealth of their master. The role model to reject is the lazy servant who hides away the money entrusted to him. Commentators on this passage have deduced many morals from this passage, such as Christians need to take risks, show courage and eschew cowardice, not to fear failure, and take advantage of opportunities or else be judged harshly by God (Herzog 1994, pp. 152-3).

However, Liberation Theologian William R. Herzog makes a strong case for an entirely different reading of the parable. According to Herzog, the first two servants are following in the master's footsteps and multiplying his wealth through burdening peasants with ruinous levels of interest, as usury was the only way such profits could be made in the ancient world. The third servant takes out of circulation the money which condemns peasants to misery, and courageously stands up to his master by identifying "the aristocrat for what he is, strict, cruel, harsh and merciless" (Herzog 1994, p. 164) whose greed impoverishes others.

The parable thus becomes a critique of a perverted form of stewardship characterising part of the economic order of the time, and that the righteous path is to identify the evil and refuse to participate in injurious stewardship activities. This interpretation forces us to acknowledge that what we think of as faithful stewardship is actually loyalty to a system which maintains and enhances wealth, privilege and power at the cost of the poor. It is better, despite the personal cost, to be 'unproductive' in such an economic order.

Application to our present greed-induced environmental crisis would have us refusing to participate in activities enriching ourselves and others that bring about environmental destruction.

The economics of enough

While the alternative reading of the parable of the talents addresses the issue of stewardship sliding from wise use to misuse and abuse, we must also look to the Scriptures to ask the question when does stewardship move from wise use to overuse.

Ched Myers (2001) has examined the signposts throughout Scriptures signaling that God's people must stop at enough, what Myers calls the practice of sabbath economics. The following are some of those signposts.

God institutes the day of rest in Genesis 1, the Hebrews' wilderness experience, and in the Ten Commandments. On the day of rest there are specific prohibitions against working the land and animals (Exodus 20:8-11, Exodus 35:2, Deuteronomy 12-15).

God restricts consumption in the manna economy of the wilderness, where collecting too much manna and storing it is pointless as the excess manna rots, except for the day before the day of rest.

God sets limits on the use of the land via the sabbath year (Leviticus 25:1-5). The seventh month of the seventh year ushered in the *Shmitah* year. God told the Hebrews, among other things, to rest the land – in fact, not to reap or harvest. This set substantial limits on production and accumulation. The meaning of the word *Shmitah* is to stretch out your hand, with anything in your hand released as a result. This is a way to describe releasing control of the land.

The decimation of Israel was related to Israel's failure to observe sabbath economics.

> [Nebuchadnezzar] carried into exile to Babylon the remnant, who escaped from the sword, and they became servants to him and his sons until the kingdom of Persia came to power. The land enjoyed its sabbath rests; all the time of its desolation it rested, until the seventy years were completed in fulfilment of the word of the LORD spoken by Jeremiah (2 Chronicles 36:20-21).

Jesus upheld the economy of enough in his life and teachings. For example, Myers (2001, pp. 27, 46-51) argues that Jesus' 40 day fast in the wilderness and the feeding of the 5000 is patterned after the wilderness experience and demonstrates that Jesus orients his ministry towards extolling the economics of enough. Sabbath economics is constantly referenced in the gospels, such as in Jesus' story of the wealthy but foolish man who accumulates barn after barn of grain, the Lord's prayer where Jesus' teaches only to ask for our daily bread, and the Lord's supper.

Stopping at enough fights our own inclinations towards greed, leaves something for those less fortunate, and allows Creation to rejuvenate. Embracing the economy of enough is a foil against ultimately self-serving, Creation endangering claims that wise stewardship is about stripping nature of all its treasures.

Accountability

Inherent in the stewardship model is accountability. We are accountable to God for the way in which we use what God has given us. This aspect of stewardship is underdeveloped. Reward and punishment spins on a simplistic formula (finding justification in the conventional reading of the parable of the talents) where reward goes to action, punishment to inaction. This is a dangerously superficial claim, but has sway in the evangelical community. Just as the church comprehensively studies and teaches about the moral code underpinning human to human relationships, and the link between morality and accountability to God, the church needs to pay far more attention to the moral code that humans need to adopt as we relate to Creation. adopt as we relate to Creation.

Not duty but love

If the non-conventional reading of the talents is accepted, Jesus is undermining the concept of a dutiful and hard working steward, but one that lacks empathy and love for those who are vulnerable. The stewardship motif brims with the concept of duty but duty is not the same as love. We must "go beyond notions of dutiful stewardship of resources to a relationship of co-responsiveness, intimacy, communion, fellowship and love ..." (Walsh, Karsh and Ansell in McDougall 2003, p.86).

Converting our hearts

Let us hold Creation as sacred, be servants (rather than managers), be the humble servant who hides away (conserves, restores and renews) nature rather than arrogantly using it up as an entitlement, an absurd service to God.

The silences of stewardship

There are two gaping silences in the stewardship motif that must be addressed in order for Creation to take up its rightful place at the heart of gospel.

Cosmic redemption

Stewardship does not capture the common history and shared destiny of human and non-human Creation in the salvific story. Non-human Creation is a key actor that seems to have been written out of the evangelical script retelling the story of the fall, salvation and redemption. McDougall reminds us that we need "to recover, in contemporary terms, the three-fold ordering of relations: God, humanity and the world" (2003, p. 117).

Young (1994) returns to the Scriptures to discover all of Creation takes a key part in this drama. Before the fall humans are in a perfect, harmonious relationship with God and the rest of Creation. When Eve and Adam disobey, not only is the relationship between God and humans broken, but also between humans and Creation. The land no longer easily yields to humans, and there is violence and bloodshed.

Creation groans for liberation from the curse that humans have brought into Creation as a result of their sin. Young stresses the innocence of non-human Creation that is incapable of sin and has not fallen, but nevertheless suffers.

The Epistles make it clear that as part of the future story of salvation, Creation will be restored and made new. Young dismisses claims that humans do not need to care for the earth because it will be destroyed to be replaced by a new earth, arguing instead that it will be the evil in the world (not the physical world itself) that will be destroyed (pp. 151-153).

In our present in-between state, where God's work of reconciling all things to himself is in process but not perfected, our ministry of reconciliation extends to all of Creation.

Young states that we must reject the fatalism and anti-environmentalism of the 'destroyed earth' eschatology (why bother to restore Creation when it will be destroyed anyway). Just as we are energised by Jesus' teaching that we should work towards the restoration of the kingdom of God on earth today we should also be energised towards the renewal of the earth.

Converting our hearts

We ourselves can begin the project in our own lives of re-situating the stories of Creation and the Christ so that they sit side by side in fulfilling the purposes of God. Together, the complementary stories of Creation and Incarnation reveal more richly the love, nature, and purposes of God. The table below is a tentative and incomplete attempt to demonstrate that Creation and Incarnation are two parts of the same story.

God speaks and Creation is formed from nothing (Genesis 1).	At the beginning of the book of John, John ties together Creation and the Incarnation.
	John proclaims Jesus as the Word and Jesus was at the beginning of Creation, and through Him the world is created (John 1:1-3).
	"In him God, nature, history and all human beings of all time are intertwined in a manner that we cannot fully fathom" (Balasuriya 1984, p.186).
God creates the light (Genesis 3).	After affirming Jesus as Creator, John uses "Light of the world" as a metaphor to describe Jesus (John 1:4-5).
The beginning	A new beginning

The love of God demonstrated.	The love of God demonstrated.
A self-emptying act of God.	A self-emptying act of God.
God begins the story of His own suffering and self-sacrifice.	God's ultimate acts of suffering and self-sacrifice.
God's creative love.	God's redeeming love.
Creation exhibits God's ability to transform nothing into something.	Jesus brings to humanity the call to, and power, for transformation.
God who is a spirit makes matter.	God who is a spirit becomes matter.
God enters the world – the triune God is both transcendent and immanent	God enters the world – the triune God is both transcendent and immanent.
God begins a relationship/communicates with something other than Himself.	God relates/communicates with the Other as the Other.
The divine character of God seen in Creation – the a priori experience of all people groups. God writ large.	The divine character of God seen in Jesus. God writ human scale.
Non-human Creation is good as it fulfills the purposes of God.	God and nature in harmony, with Jesus commanding and non-human Creation obeying.
The motif of abundance – God's desire for all Creation to live a life of sufficiency in a world of plenty.	The motif of the abundant life – God's desire for all to live an abundant life. Jesus teachings would allow for the economic and social changes that would return everyone to a life of sufficiency in a world of plenty.
The suffering of Creation which is innocent, due to human sin.	The suffering of Christ who is innocent, due to human sin.

The distribution of Creation's abundance

Brueggemann (1999) pronounces Genesis 1 as a liturgy of abundance.

> The Bible starts out with a liturgy of abundance. Genesis 1 is a song of praise for God's generosity. It tells how well the world is ordered. It keeps saying, "It is good, it is good, it is good, it is very good." It declares that God blesses – that is, endows with vitality – the plants and the animals and the fish and the birds and humankind. And it pictures the creator as saying, "Be fruitful and multiply." In an orgy of fruitfulness, everything in its kind is to multiply the overflowing goodness that pours from God's creator spirit. And as you know, the creation ends in Sabbath. God is so overrun with fruitfulness that God says, "I've got to take a break from all this. I've got to get out of the office."

As previously shown, the Bible constantly reaffirms that God has provided more than enough for everyone, as long as we put reasonable limits on what we take from the earth.

Our unprecedented environmental crisis combines with humanitarian tragedies due, in significant part, to some humans and human communities taking more than their share of the earth's bounty. Stewardship alone does not provide a political and economic analysis to reveal the rampant exploitation of one human community over another and the devastating outcomes that result for the human and environmental victims.

Theft, exploitation and oppression have come in many guises. People groups have been allocated the lands on which they live.

> From one man he made every nation of men, that they should inhabit the whole earth; and he determined the times set for them and the exact places where they should live (Acts 17:26).

Human groups have violated the divine allocation of land through the ages, but never on such a massive scale as colonial times when nations stole whole land masses from other groups, as happened for example, to the Indigenous nations of Australia. Uniformly, dispossessed peoples with a very benign relationship to the land were conquered by people groups whose aggressive industrialised forms of agriculture and resource extraction ravaged homelands.

Other forms of environmental theft and looting have been conducted under the pretext of trade. Our rapacious appetite for material goods, normalised by the dominant consumer narrative and enabled by globalisation, means that we co-operate in the destruction of particular ecosystems providing for the physical, cultural and spiritual nourishment of people groups we do not even know exist, simply with the swipe of our MasterCard. Nahum could be talking about the modern trading system instead of denouncing Nineveh's exploitative trading practices when he says "You have increased the number of your merchants till they are more than the stars of the sky, but like locusts they strip the land and then fly away" (Nahum 3:16).

Examples of this are commonplace, one example here will suffice. Cornford (2009) tells the story of the Phnong ethnic minority group in Sambor District, Cambodia. Over a period of two years the people group has been forced into a marginal existence due to "lost forest and cultivated land to three different commercial plantations (for rubber and teak)". Many have probably benefited from this resource exploitation: plantation owners, traders, the Cambodian Government, distributors, retailers, consumers of rubber and teak. But the land of the group whose place and natural wealth was, we may assume, determined by God, has been pillaged.

The appalling failure of the developed countries to address carbon pollution levels that they are largely responsible for creating, also represents a type of theft of lands. From the village of Shishmaref in North Alaska, to the Carteret Islands in the South Pacific, homelands designated by God are literally disappearing, or are being made unlivable (through, for example, salination of the water supply), due to the effects of climate change.

While the stewardship ethic in itself does not provide a way to explain and mobilise action against the unfair exploitation and marginalisation of the poor, and the implication for the environment, the Scriptures resound in observing and speaking out against evil doers who evict peasants from the land assigned to them by God, their source of economic freedom and social position.

Fair distribution of land in Israel was the cornerstone of economic freedom, justice and equality. Stephen Mott reminds us that God intended the society to be egalitarian in nature, existing as "freeholding peasants who had similar resources in orchards, pastures, and habitations" as a result of the allocation of land which would be inherited, held in perpetuity and unsaleable (1982, pp. 65, 66).

Hebrew society failed to uphold egalitarian principles, with greed driving sinful accumulation of landholdings, resulting in homelessness and lost inheritance.

> Woe to those who plan iniquity,
> to those who plot evil on their beds!
> At morning's light they carry it out
> because it is in their power to do it.
> They covet fields and seize them,
> and houses, and take them.
> They defraud a man of his home,
> a fellowman of his inheritance.
> Therefore, the LORD says:
> "I am planning disaster against this people,
> from which you cannot save yourselves.
> You will no longer walk proudly,
> for it will be a time of calamity"
> (Micah 2:1-3).

> The LORD enters into judgment
> against the elders and leaders of his people:
> "It is you who have ruined my vineyard;
> the plunder from the poor is in your houses.
> What do you mean by crushing my people
> and grinding the faces of the poor?"
> declares the Lord, the LORD Almighty
> (Isaiah 3:14-15).

Mott says by the eighth century BC:

> Through mortgage foreclosing and oppressive share cropping arrangements, the peasants lost their heritage from the Lord and their economic and social position. They were disappearing as an independent class, many even passing into slavery (1982, p. 66).

Clearly God's expectation is that we do not deprive individuals and people groups of their land and livelihoods.

Converting our hearts

Our notion of stewardship must be expanded to recognise the centrality of land in God's plans of economic justice and freedom, as clearly found in Scriptures. We must do our best to see through the consumer-centred economic ethic of our time to the injustice that it causes as the capacity of land allocated to people groups to meet their needs is stolen from them, to meet our insatiable appetite for stuff.

Conclusion: Reframing the stewardship ethic

Mounting an argument against stewardship feels like questioning the Trinity. The word Trinity is not used in the Bible, but it has become one of the cornerstones of the Christian faith. Stewardship was never a term directly applied by any of the Bible's authors to our relationship with the environment but it now dominates our understanding of the way we ought to relate to the physical world.

Unfortunately the stewardship stance has been too aligned with the worldview that it is the destiny of humans to display our mastery of the environment. The evangelical church has lost the opportunity to be a prophetic voice to the world, instead seen (fairly or unfairly) as a source of violence to rather than healing of Creation. Now we can only hope to play catch up and be accepted as a voice mobilising Christians to engage in the wider environmental movement.

The pulpit, the liturgy and worship service, the home group, the Sunday school class, the elders' meeting, the church property committee are all places where we can at least influence congregations to change their orientation and rethink the lifestyles with a reinterpreted, reformed, richer, conception of stewardship. Or perhaps stewardship has been so weakened and distorted that new metaphors must take centre stage in the work of renewing our minds and re-imagining our relationship with Creation through serious Biblical reflection that continues beyond the first 28 verses of the Bible.

The following table is a simplified and tentative proposal on how the stewardship metaphor could be reshaped. The proposal sees us moving from the language of *owners to tenants, raw materials to sacred places, masters of Creation to servants of Creation, the pinnacle of creation to interdependent with Creation, control over to a special mission within.* As David Power says, we need metaphors that "dissolve the domineering tendencies of man over man, of man over woman, of humanity over the cosmos and allow us to hear the voice between the cracks" (in McDougall 2003, p. 125).

Stewardship weakened and marginalised by egocentric/anthropocentric theologies and secular ideologies	Re-forming stewardship	Replacing stewardship as the dominant evangelical conception of our relationship with non-human Creation
Non-human Creation divorced from and devoid of God.	Non-human Creation bearing God's imprint, awash with praise for God, intimately sustained by God, instrument of revelation, loved by God.	*Creation is sacred* and we must observe taboos that recognise our limited understanding of the mystery of God's relationship with non-human Creation, the mystery of the workings of eco systems and our limited understanding of the consequences of our actions.
God has ceded control of the earth to humanity. King, governor, and vice-regent connotations of stewardship.	Creation only continues to exist through God's creative, sustaining involvement as Creator and owner of the Universe. Humans have a limited, conditional role. We are *tenants* on God's land. *Servants* and *slaves* are metaphors just as legitimate as kings, governors and vice regents in depicting the role God has given us.	Experiment with models of property ownership that are more consistent with the Biblical imperative to see ourselves as tenants only.
Humans are the pinnacle/apex of Creation. Created order/Chain of being.	The seventh day (not the sixth when humans are created) is the pinnacle of Creation – God sees the everything made	Shalom (all things in harmony) and servanthood become the dominant motif to replace stewardship as characterising the significance of the human role relative to the rest of Creation.

		significance of the human role relative to the rest of Creation.
	out of nothing as the pinnacle of His creative acts. Humans need to appreciate our common life with the rest of Creation, humbly recognise the suffering of Creation as a result of human sin, serve rather than place Creation in servitude, acknowledge the interdependence of all species. Kinship/ Web of life/ Mutuality/ Repentance/ Reconciliation	
Creation a resource to use, with use (rather than letting things be) bringing glory to God.	Put limits on use. Economics of enough. Trustees, custodians, protectors other potential metaphors.	*Live sacrificially* as a prophetic voice.
	Duty to Creation	Sacrificial love of Creation.
Stewardship must settle for also-ran status. The story of human redemption cannot share the stage with any other narrative.		Reinstate the metanarrative of Creation as just as significant in our spiritual journey as the redemption story.
Lacks political and economic analysis and prophetic call for justice.	Analyse and advocate against injustice.	Live radically differently and centrestage social, economic and ecological justice as the heart of the gospel, alongside spiritual reformation.

References

Balasuriya, T. (1984). *Planetary theology*. Maryknoll, NY: Orbis Books.

Brueggemann, W. (1997). *Theology of the Old Testament: Testimony, dispute, advocacy*. Minneapolis, MN: Fortress Press.

Brueggemann, W. (1999). *The liturgy of abundance, the myth of scarcity*. Retrieved January 6, 2010 from http://www.religion-online.org/showarticle.asp?title=533

Cornford, J. (2009). Who are the poor and what do they really want? *Manna Matters*, November, 4-7.

Donovan, V.J. (1989). *The church in the midst of creation*. Maryknoll, NY: Orbis Books.

Douglas, S. (2009). Religious environmentalism in the West: I. A focus on Christianity. *Religion Compass*, 3/4, 717-737.

Dowd, M. (2007). *God is green*. BBC Channel 4.

Gibson, J. (2007). Communities out of place. In C.A. Maida (Ed.), *Sustainability and communities of place* (pp. 63-81). Oxford: Berghahn Books.

Goodall, J. (1971). *In the shadow of man*. Boston: Houghton Mifflin.

Hall, D.J. (1986). *Imaging God: Dominion as stewardship*. Eugene, OR: Wipf and Stock Publishers.

Herzog, W.R. (1994). *Parables as subversive speech: Jesus as pedagogue of the oppressed.* Louisville, KY: Westminster/John Knox Press.

Hiebert, T. (1996). Rethinking dominion theology. *Directions,* 25(2), 16-25. http://www.directionjournal.org/article/?922.

Lester, J. (2008). Indigenous belonging – Our heritage. *National Trust Magazine,* 6, 22-23.

McDougall, D.C. (2003). *The cosmos as the primary sacrament: The horizon for an ecological sacramental theology.* New York: Peter Lang Publishing.

Mott, S.C. (1982). *Biblical ethics and social change.* New York: Oxford University Press.

Myers, C. (2001). *The Biblical vision of Sabbath economics.* Washington, DC: The Church of the Saviour.

Tubbs, J.B., Jr. (1994). Humble dominion. *Theology Today,* 50, 543-556. http://theologytoday.ptsem.edu/jan1994/v50-4-article4.htm

White, L., Jr. (1967). The historical roots of our ecological crisis. *Science,* 155, 1203-1207.

Wilkinson, L. (1991). *Earthkeeping in the nineties: Stewardship of creation.* Eugene, OR: Wipf and Stock Publishers.

Young, R.A. (1994). *Healing the earth: A theocentric perspective on environmental problems and their solutions.* Nashville, TN: Broadman & Holman.

www.ingramcontent.com/pod-product-compliance
Lightning Source LLC
Chambersburg PA
CBHW051633230426
43669CB00013B/2281